Cases of Nevada's Gaming Commission

Decades of over 100 real-life Gambling Violations

Cases of Nevada's Gaming Commission

Decades of over 100 real-life Gambling Violations

By

Sandi Jerome

SmilingEagle Press Book

1st Edition

Published by SmilingEagle Press
For information:
SmilingEagle Press
1071 Edgewood Ave South Suite 102
Jacksonville, FL 92205
www.smilingeagle.com

Printed in the United States of America

Cover Design by: Nilesh Prabhu
author.nileshprabhu@gmail.com

Dedication

This book is dedicated to my fearless women warriors; Chandra, Suby, Tulaasi and Vrinda who have made my life an adventure and my husband Keith who has taken the ride with me.

A special dedication to my father, Larry Cook who inspired this book and love gambling. His best times are in a casino, even today!

Cases of Nevada's Gaming Commission

Decades of over 100 Cases

Contents

Introduction

I grew up in a gambling family. My mom's wedding advice was, "If he's a drunk, make sure you're on the barstool next to him and if he's a gambler, be at the next slot machine." Mom used to tell the story how they'd have poker night every Saturday and at church the next day, when the collection basket was passed by, my brother and I would say, "Bet ya a dime, or I'll raise you a quarter!"

We'd go "camping" a few times a year to Las Vegas. It was a 5-hour drive from Escondido, where I grew up, and my parents would take our camper and stay at the RV park at Circus Circus. For us, that was almost as exciting as Disneyland which we spent our other free time because my grandmother lives a few blocks away and some of the land that Disneyland sits on was once owned by my great-grandmother.

Las Vegas is our playground. I learned how to ski on one ski in Lake Mead. I've been to see Celine, Phil Collins, and Mama Mia. My husband once surprised me on our first anniversary. We had dinner at the iconic Anthony's Fish Grotto at San Diego's harbor. Sadly Anthony's which was founded by Catherine "Mama" Ghio in 1946 sailed into the sunset on January 31, 2017.

But getting back to that anniversary dinner, we had watched the planes landing at San Diego's airport during the meal and my husband said, "Let's go to Las Vegas!" I was pregnant at the time and thinking the fun days were almost over, I replied, "I'm all in!"

At this time in the early 1970s, PSA - Pacific Southwest Airlines flew on the hour to Las Vegas and it was cheap, only about the cost of our "expensive" dinner at about $20. Off we went to Las Vegas and it was a shock to see that the NADA convention was in town. I didn't realize how big the car business was and how big it would factor into my life later.

We wandered around town seeing all the "Welcome NADA Car Dealers," at every hotel and they were sold out. I called my best friend, Laura, who worked for Hughes Air West in Las Vegas (the big banana) and there was no answer and this was before cell phones.

I figured that I better call my mother and let her know and get some suggestions for a hotel that might not be filled with celebrating car dealers. When she answered, it was more of a shriek than anything else. The next day for our anniversary, she and my best friend who had driven out from Las Vegas, were throwing a combined anniversary and baby shower for me-in Escondido. My mom insisted we grab the next PSA flight home.

We made it home in time and the party was a success, along with my career in the car business. I had started when I was fourteen because my neighbor was a parts manager at the local Buick dealership and they kept the parts inventory on little 3x5 cards; one for each part. I'd go in with my dashing sixteen-year-old neighbor, Danah, who was the object of my teen crush, and work updating the part inventory.

Later, while in college, I worked my way up at a huge San Diego dealership, Courtesy Chevrolet, I was there for the first posting machine's arrival and then for the first computer that calculated finance contracts. Over the next few years, I went part time to college, getting my accounting degree with a minor in computer science and becoming a finance manager, and eventually a CFO.

At the same time, my husband worked his way through the nuclear industry, first for the Department of Defense at NAS North Island

and then into the private industry, becoming a technical writer at Diablo Canyon Nuclear Generating Station in California's beautiful central coast.

We had it made, a house on the ocean in Shell Beach and I found a Ford Dealership in Pismo Beach that need a CFO to take them through a computer conversion. I had recently earned my CPA certificate, and Danny Pace hired me saying, "That's worth an extra grand a month." Thank goodness because it has cost me a lot to pay my own way through college and then obtain my CPA.

One problem; Danny Pace of ran a bookie service out of the dealership. I had only worked there a few weeks until I realized that things were odd. The first sign was the safe. It was filled with cash. Normally a dealership only keeps about $500 in cash, but there were stacks and stacks of it and none of it showed on the books.

Next, I noticed a gun in Danny's bottom drawer. Shocked, I asked why he kept a gun at the dealership. He insisted it was necessary, but I told him it was unacceptable. Disagreements are common between accountants and their bosses, and I didn't want him to get angry and pull a gun on me. He ended up locking it up in the safe.

Although the dealer was weird, I like the job; I was learning the new Ford computer system and making friends. In fact one of the ladies that worked for me, Tammy, and I became good friends and she later visited us in Hawaii where I ended my dealership career as the CFO of a group of dealership. Tammy eventually went to work for the state DMV in Sacramento – and even got to meet Arnold when he was governor. We stayed in touch until she died a few years ago.

My son was having trouble fitting in - but eventually he found a nerdy kid like himself that liked to ride the surf together. On the day my son brought his newly found friend came by after school, we got a surprise raid from the FBI. About a dozen agents with the dark windbreakers and big FBI letters took up positions throughout the dealership. They refused to let anyone come or go. My son and his friend were in the meeting room doing homework, waiting for a ride to the beach, and I asked to talk to the agent in charge. I explained that I had only worked there a few months and truly didn't know anything other than there was a gun and lots of cash in the safe. They asked if I could talk Danny Pace into coming back to the dealership, but I replied that I was the last person who could talk him into coming in.

After opening the safe for the FBI, the agent let me leave with the kids. Before leaving, I packed up the few personal items in my desk, because I had no intention of returning to work for this guy. After taking the boys to the beach, I went home, and the next day the racketeering bust was on the front page. Danny was a bookie, taking gambling bets, then flying to Las Vegas on his private plane to place them for his clients. Since Keith was making a lot of money at the nuclear power plant, I decided to be a stay home mom.

I had been working a lot with a spreadsheet and Lotus 1-2-3 and decided to write a book, "Lotus 1-2-3 for Small Business." I sent out the proposal to a couple publishers and a week later got a call that Compute! Books wanted to publish my book. I had previously written a book with a partner, Quick-Start Guide for 12 top PC Programs, but that we had self-published and sold out of a computer store in Arizona.

Compute! was a real "listed" publisher, and I got a nice advance. I used it to buy a laser printer. At this time, laser printers cost more than a couple month's house payments, so it was a major investment for me, and a delightful upgrade from dot matrix printer which printed on rolls of tan paper with holes on each side.

Fast forward to today. I'm still writing and have written dozens of books and I later left the car business and wrote accounting and factory integration software for the industry. I merged my company into a bigger one and took their stock and a moderate monthly check in return. Now, I'm living my dream of writing full time and after graduating from UCLA's Advanced Screenwriting program, I branched out into screenplays. You can read more about that in my bio at the end.

While I was transiting from the car business to technology, I found I had a knack for accounting forensics. I can quickly scan transactions and see things that don't look right.

I once gave a seminar at the AICPA's annual conference called "*Catch Me if You Can*," somewhat based on a book I had recently read that would later become a popular movie with Leonardo DiCaprio. The seminar is the only one of mine over the years that is not available on DVD from their library because they were worried that I was giving CFOs too many ideas. I thought that was silly until years later, Patricia K. Smith, a controller like I was, stole over ten million and was sentenced to three years and had to pay it back.

When researching Las Vegas theft for a screenplay I was developing into a TV series, I discovered Nevada's Gaming Commission. I've watched "outliner" levels of crime shows, but couldn't remember anything about this agency. Thus, I started this book. It is more of a reference guide, a starting point for you to find some cases that seem interesting. There are over a hundred to pick from and maybe you'll find the next "Oceans 42" movie idea. As I finish up this book, I understand a prequel is in production! But first, let's look at this agency with a little history.

History of Nevada's Gaming Commission

Today's Gaming Commission (NGC) and its investigative arm, the Nevada Gaming Control Board (NGCB), stand as the gold standard for gaming regulation worldwide. Established in 1959, these agencies oversee one of the world's largest gaming markets. Its history reflects Nevada's transformation from a frontier state with unregulated gambling to the gold standard of gaming control.

The Early Years: 1931-1955

When Nevada legalized gambling in 1931, during the Great Depression, the industry operated with minimal oversight. Local law enforcement handled gaming matters, leading to inconsistent enforcement and allowing organized crime to gain a foothold in casino operations. Tax collection was irregular, and there were no standardized regulations for gaming operations.

Birth of Modern Regulation: 1955-1959

The modern era of gaming regulation began in 1955 with the creation of the Nevada Gaming Control Board (NGCB), established under the Nevada Tax Commission. This marked the state's first serious attempt at centralizing gaming oversight. However, it quickly became apparent that a more comprehensive regulatory framework was needed.

In 1959, the Nevada Legislature passed the Gaming Control Act, establishing the Nevada Gaming Commission as the state's ultimate gaming regulatory authority. This pivotal legislation created the two-tier system still in use today:

1. The Gaming Control Board: Handles day-to-day oversight and investigations
2. The Nevada Gaming Commission: Makes final decisions on licensing and regulatory matters

The Hughes Era: 1960s-1970s

The 1960s brought significant changes as the Commission worked to eliminate organized crime from the casino industry. Howard Hughes's arrival in Las Vegas in 1966 marked a turning point, as his corporate approach to casino ownership helped legitimize the industry. The Commission actively supported this transition from mob-connected individuals to corporate ownership.

Strengthening Oversight: 1970s-1980s

During this period, the Commission implemented several groundbreaking regulatory measures:

1. The Corporate Gaming Act (1969): Allowed publicly traded companies to own casinos
2. Creation of the List of Excluded Persons ("Black Book") - see the last chapter.
3. Implementation of strict accounting and auditing requirements
4. Development of comprehensive licensing investigations

Evolving Challenges - 1990s-Present

The Commission has continued to evolve, addressing new challenges:

- - Regulation of electronic gaming devices and systems
- - Overview of online gaming operations
- - Implementation of responsible gaming initiatives
- - Development of regulations for cashless gaming systems
- - Oversight of mobile sports betting platforms

The Nevada Gaming Commission now manages:

1. Licensing decisions for gaming establishments
2. Adoption of regulations and standards
3. Disciplinary actions against license holders
4. Final approval of gaming devices and systems
5. Setting industry policy

The NGC's regulatory framework has been emulated by jurisdictions worldwide, from New Jersey to Macau. Its emphasis on strict oversight while allowing for industry innovation has proven crucial to Nevada's gaming industry success. The Commission's standards have helped establish Nevada as the global leader in gaming regulation.

The Gaming Commission Today

As gaming continues to evolve with technological advances and changing consumer preferences, the Nevada Gaming Commission faces four new challenges:

1. Regulation of cryptocurrency in gaming
2. Oversight of skill-based gaming devices

3. Integration of artificial intelligence in gaming operations
4. Balance between innovation and consumer protection

The Commission's ability to adapt while maintaining strict regulatory standards remains crucial to the continued success of Nevada's gaming with unique hiring practices and operational structures designed to maintain the integrity of Nevada's gaming industry.

The NGC consists of five part-time commissioners appointed by the governor, while the NGCB operates with three full-time board members. The NGCB handles the day-to-day regulatory operations and employs the majority of the agencies' workforce.

The NGCB maintains strict hiring requirements for its gaming agents:

- ✓ Minimum of a bachelor's degree in accounting, business administration, finance, or related fields
- ✓ Clean criminal record
- ✓ Nevada residency requirements after hiring
- ✓ Extensive background checks including financial history
- ✓ Mandatory drug testing and ongoing screening

To continue working for the NGCB, an agent must maintain:

- ✓ Nevada gaming employee registration
- ✓ Valid driver's license
- ✓ Ability to work flexible schedules including nights and weekends
- ✓ Willingness to travel throughout Nevada

Does this sound like fun? During their new agent 6-month probationary period, agents experience and learn through intensive training:

- Gaming laws and regulations
- Casino operations and game protection
- Investigative techniques
- Financial analysis and auditing procedures

As of 2024, the agencies employ approximately:
- 400 total employees
- 95 sworn agents
- 80 auditors
- Support staff including IT specialists, legal counsel, and administrative personnel

The Nevada Gaming Agencies are self-funded through:
- Gaming license fees
- Gaming device taxes
- Penalties and fines

Annual budget highlights:
- Operating budget of approximately $50 million
- Majority allocated to personnel costs
- Significant investment in technology and training
- Revenue generation exceeding operational costs

Divisions and Responsibilities

Enforcement Division
- Conducts criminal and regulatory investigations
- Monitors gaming operations
- Responds to patron complaints
- Performs background checks

Audit Division
- Reviews financial statements
- Conducts compliance audits
- Monitors internal controls

- Analyzes revenue reports

Technology Division
- Tests and certifies gaming devices
- Evaluates casino surveillance systems
- Monitors gaming software
- Oversees cybersecurity measures

Impact and Jurisdiction
The agencies oversee:
- Over 400 licensed casinos
- Over 2,000 licensed gaming locations
- Approximately 140,000 slot machines
- Over 50,000 gaming employees

The Nevada Gaming Commission and Gaming Control Board maintain their effectiveness through selective hiring practices, comprehensive training, and adequate funding. Their model has been replicated by gaming jurisdictions worldwide, demonstrating the success of their regulatory approach and employment standards. Here are some of the cases. I only list the original complaint since these are cases that I want to investigate further for my TV show, but I think you can see the wide variety of topics. Enjoy!

The Cases

Boomtown Reno – Play Online Violations

Between March and August 2017, Boomtown Reno's official website featured "Play Online" and "Play Even When Away!" links directing visitors to 15 different online gaming options. Eleven of these links led to real-money gambling websites operated by Affiliate Edge and Deck Media, both based in Curacao.

The Nevada Gaming Control Board launched an investigation after receiving complaints from patrons questioning the legality of these online gaming offerings. On August 17, 2017, a Board agent contacted Boomtown about the illegal nature of the links.

The investigation revealed three of the real-money gambling sites displayed Boomtown advertisements. Several sites openly advertised themselves as "US Friendly," "US Players Welcome," or "US Friendly Casino," complete with American flag graphics.

Financial records showed Boomtown received payments through these arrangements. The casino collected a $1,621.03 check from Affiliate Edge via Evo Advertising, Inc. Account statements confirmed gambling activity by Boomtown-referred players and related commission payments from both Affiliate Edge and Deck Media.

The Board cited Boomtown for operating without an interactive gaming license and enabling apparent violations of both state law and the federal Wire Act, which prohibits interstate transmission of wagers.

A second count revealed serious oversight failures. The Board found Boomtown had delegated complete control of its website's gaming links to a single employee - a graphic and web designer with limited understanding of gaming laws. The casino reportedly exercised minimal supervision over the employee's actions.

The complaint highlighted Boomtown's failure to investigate these links even after receiving payments from the websites and a patron's inquiry about their legality. The Board argued these acts and omissions reflected poorly on Nevada's gaming industry and constituted unsuitable operation methods.

The Nevada Gaming Commission will determine potential fines and disciplinary actions against Boomtown's gaming license.

CG Technology Hit with Multiple Violations

The Nevada Gaming Control Board filed a complaint against CG Technology Holdings and its subsidiaries for multiple violations spanning from 2016 to 2018, marking another round of regulatory troubles for the sports betting operator.

The complaint outlines four major counts of violations, beginning with CG Technology's failure to prevent out-of-state wagering. In November 2016, a patron placed a sports bet while physically located in Maryland. Despite implementing software modifications after this incident, the company's inadequate deployment led to seven more out-of-state wagers in April 2017, with bets coming from Texas, Arizona, and California.

In a second count, the Board cited CG Technology for accepting wagers after sporting events had concluded. On October 1, 2016, the company allowed 33 wagers from 14 patrons on an NCAA football game after its completion. A similar incident occurred on October

14, 2017, when nine patrons placed bets on another NCAA football game after it ended.

The third count revealed a programming flaw in CG Technology's betting system dating back to August 2011. The error affected 1,483 winning wagers, resulting in 783 patrons receiving $7,368 more than expected while 700 others got $4,465 less than their due. The flaw occurred when bets were placed at the exact moment prices were being updated.

The final count involved a misconfigured satellite sports betting station during a Super Bowl party on February 4, 2018. The station was set up in a testing environment instead of the live production environment, leading to 14 wagers being placed with incorrect odds. Eleven of these bets had different point spreads or total over-under lines compared to the company's standard offerings.

The regulatory action follows previous disciplinary measures against CG Technology, including a 2016 complaint regarding similar violations. The Board seeks monetary fines for each violation and potential action against the company's licenses, registrations, and findings of suitability.

CG Technology operates sports books at several prominent Las Vegas locations, including The M Resort, Hard Rock Hotel & Casino, Tropicana, Cosmopolitan, Venetian, Palms, and Silverton Casino Lodge.

Bally's Poker Dealer - $5 Chips Theft

A poker dealer at Bally's Las Vegas faces revocation of his gaming employee registration after allegedly stealing chips from the casino rake. Jesus Saucedo was observed taking a $5 chip from the casino's rake box and placing it in his personal toke box on June 17, 2017.

The Nevada Gaming Control Board filed a complaint detailing how a Bally's Surveillance Agent caught Saucedo in the act. Further investigation of surveillance footage revealed two additional instances where Saucedo diverted $5 chips from the casino's rake into his personal toke box.

Following the discovery, Bally's Director of Security signed an Arrest by Private Person form, and Saucedo signed a Misdemeanor Citation/Complaint.

The Gaming Control Board seeks to revoke Saucedo's gaming employee registration under Nevada Revised Statutes 463.337(2), which permits revocation if an employee commits, attempts, or conspires to commit larceny or embezzlement against a gaming licensee or on licensed gaming premises.

The case, filed in October 2017, will proceed to a hearing before the Nevada Gaming Commission, where Saucedo will have an opportunity to respond to the allegations. If found in violation, he could lose his ability to work in Nevada's gaming industry.

Bally's Las Vegas, operated by Parball Newco, LLC, holds a nonrestricted gaming license in Nevada.

Casinos Charged with Sports Betting Violations

The Nevada Gaming Control Board filed a complaint against Station Casinos LLC and NP Red Rock LLC, alleging multiple violations related to their sports betting operations between 2018 and 2021.

According to the complaint, Red Rock Casino Resort Spa accepted approximately 348 sports wagers on events after their outcomes had already been determined. The violations occurred through the casino's mobile sports wagering application, which used the Stadium Live program.

The first incident happened in June 2018, when Red Rock accepted money for about 35 sports wagers on five events after they had ended. The Board issued a violation letter, citing computer errors related to insufficient server memory in the Stadium Live program.

A more significant breach occurred in January 2019, when the mobile app accepted 116 wagers on completed events. A Station's employee confirmed these server failures were "100 percent avoidable." The pattern continued in March 2019, with 30 more illegal wagers accepted on at least three finished events.

The Board issued an Order to Show Cause in August 2019, requiring Station Casinos to explain why a complaint should not be filed. Despite the casino's response and supplemental filing, problems persisted.

In March 2021, Red Rock reported another malfunction, resulting in 167 sports wagering tickets written for completed events. The casino refunded and voided these tickets, but the damage was done.

The complaint outlines two counts against Station Casinos. Count One alleges violations of Nevada gaming regulations, particularly the requirement prohibiting tickets from being written after an event's outcome is known. Count Two focuses on the casino's failure to maintain sufficient control and monitoring processes for their mobile sports wagering application.

The Gaming Board seeks monetary fines for each violation and potential action against Station Casinos' licenses. The complaint emphasizes the regulators had previously warned the company to implement "redundant monitoring processes" to prevent accepting wagers on completed events.

The case highlights Nevada's strict oversight of gaming operations and the state's commitment to maintaining public confidence in the industry through rigorous regulation of gaming establishments.

William Hill - Duplicate Wagers

The Nevada Gaming Control Board filed a complaint against William Hill U.S. Holdco and its subsidiaries for multiple violations spanning from 2015 through 2022, including system flaws causing erroneous duplicate wagers and inadequate customer service.

In June 2021, patrons complained to William Hill about erroneous duplicate wagers occurring through their CBS Race and Sports Book System. The company discovered the issue but failed to notify the Gaming Board, instead implementing a "system patch" to address the problem. The Board only learned of the issue in September 2021 through a patron dispute.

An internal investigation by William Hill revealed approximately 42,000 erroneous duplicate losing wagers in Nevada, resulting in patron losses of $1.3 million. Additionally, about 13,000 erroneous duplicate winning wagers led to patrons winning approximately $2 million. The issue dated back to 2015.

The company's investigation determined the duplications occurred during peak traffic times due to a system flaw. When the system was under heavy load, impatient patrons would exit and retry their wagers, leading to multiple processing of the same bet once the system stabilized.

In a separate issue, the Board received numerous complaints throughout 2021 regarding William Hill's customer service. The situation worsened in January 2022 when the company terminated phone and chat support due to staffing issues, forcing all customer service to email only. The Board noted the volume of complaints was "unreasonable and excessive."

A third violation occurred when William Hill Sports Book at Red Garter Hotel & Casino failed to promptly report a $3,350 cash shortage discovered on April 12, 2022. A sportsbook writer had allegedly made unlawful wagers using money from their bank drawer. The company waited until May 12 to notify the Board's Elko Enforcement office, despite receiving a previous violation letter in December 2021 for a similar reporting delay.

The Gaming Board seeks monetary fines and potential action against William Hill's licenses, registrations, and findings of suitability for these violations.

Family Food Mart Partnership -Drug Sales

The Nevada Gaming Control Board filed a complaint against Family Food Mart Partnership in Las Vegas, alleging the restricted gaming licensee allowed methamphetamine sales inside its establishment on multiple occasions in June 2021.

According to the complaint, the Las Vegas Metropolitan Police Department received numerous complaints about illegal drug sales at the Fremont Street location in May 2021, prompting an investigation.

In late June, police used a confidential informant to make two separate drug purchases inside the gaming area. During the first transaction, the informant spoke a code phrase to a cashier, who directed them to a person sitting at a slot machine. The informant purchased 0.62 grams of methamphetamine from the individual.

A week later, the same process led to another purchase of 1.36 grams of methamphetamine. The informant reported the second transaction occurred in full view of the cashier, with no attempt to conceal the illegal activity.

The Board's complaint cites Family Food Mart for failing to prevent these activities and operating in an unsuitable manner. The violations reflect poorly on Nevada's gaming industry and constitute grounds for disciplinary action under state gaming regulations.

The Gaming Control Board seeks monetary fines for each violation and potential action against Family Food Mart's gaming license. The case highlights Nevada's strict oversight of gaming establishments and requirement to maintain suitable business operations protecting public welfare.

The complaint emphasizes the gaming industry's importance to Nevada's economy and reputation, noting licensees must prevent criminal activities and maintain proper standards of operation to preserve public confidence in the state's gaming sector.

Artesian Partners - Undisclosed Ownership Transfer

Nevada gaming regulators filed a complaint against Artesian Partners LLC, operating as Peavine Taphouse Eats and Beats, and its owners Anita Marie Noble and Matthew Todd Reardon for violating multiple gaming regulations related to an unauthorized ownership transfer.

The complaint stems from a series of transactions beginning in July 2020, when Noble and Reardon entered into a Membership Interest Purchase Agreement. Under this agreement, Noble would acquire Reardon's 50% stake in Artesian Partners for $150,000, paid in two $75,000 installments.

Noble made the first payment to Reardon in July 2020. The Commission approved Artesian Partners' restricted gaming license application in April 2021, along with Noble and Reardon as members and managers. Noble completed the second payment in June 2021, when Reardon signed over his membership interest.

The violations came to light in August 2022, when an application was finally submitted to transfer Reardon's 50% interest to Noble. This late disclosure revealed multiple regulatory breaches.

The Gaming Control Board outlined three main violations:

Count One accuses the respondents of violating regulations by exchanging payment for the ownership transfer without Commission approval or placing funds in escrow.

Count Two alleges an unauthorized transfer of interest in a gaming licensee, as Reardon purportedly transferred his stake to Noble without required advance Commission approval.

Count Three focuses on the failure to disclose the July 2020 agreement and June 2021 payment during the licensing application process, violating regulations requiring complete and updated information.

The Board seeks monetary fines for each violation and potential action against the respondents' licenses. The case highlights Nevada's strict oversight of gaming ownership changes and disclosure requirements.

The complaint emphasizes Nevada's position on gaming regulation, citing state law recognizing how "public confidence and trust can only be maintained by strict regulation of all persons, locations, practices, associations and activities related to the operation of licensed gaming establishments."

Tahoe Nugget - Employee Registration

The Nevada Gaming Control Board filed a complaint against Jim Kelley's Tahoe Nugget casino for numerous violations regarding gaming employee registrations and failure to maintain proper communication channels.

The investigation began when Board agents attempted to contact the Crystal Bay establishment in September 2022 about employee registration issues. They discovered the casino's phone number was inoperative, forcing agents to physically visit the location to make contact.

Though Tahoe Nugget secured a new phone number in October 2022, subsequent issues persisted. The casino failed to monitor its voicemail, with owner James Kelley stating messages were never checked. He told investigators people would need to contact him or his brother directly or visit in person.

The Board uncovered multiple employee registration violations. The casino hired Alesha Garcia and Jesse Ault as gaming employees in April 2022 but failed to submit their registration applications. Another employee, Adelia Stevenson, worked without proper transfer documentation from her previous employer.

Two employees, Rogelio Cruz and Brad Barnes, continued working with expired registrations. Barnes' registration lapsed in March 2021, yet he remained employed until March 2023 despite multiple notifications to management.

The investigation revealed further compliance issues. The casino failed to submit required monthly hire reports for most of 2021 and 2022. It also neglected to report employee terminations within mandated timeframes.

Additional violations emerged after the Board's initial Order to Show Cause. Jesus Cabrera worked on the count team without proper gaming registration, and Nathaniel Spitze worked as a gaming employee for four years before his registration was submitted in March 2023.

The Board cited two main counts against Tahoe Nugget: unsuitable method of operation regarding gaming employee compliance and unsuitable method of operation regarding inability to contact the establishment. These violations reflect poorly on Nevada's gaming industry and fail to meet proper operational standards, according to the complaint.

The Gaming Commission will determine potential fines and actions against Tahoe Nugget's gaming licenses. Each violation carries separate penalties under Nevada gaming regulations.

S&P Gaming - Unauthorized Share Transfers

Nevada gaming regulators filed a complaint against S&P Gaming Inc., operating as The Watering Hole in Spring Creek, Nevada, for multiple violations including unauthorized share transfers and filing false statements.

The Nevada Gaming Control Board's complaint outlines three major counts against the company and its officers Peter Lawrence Lusich III and Diane Kesler Lusich.

According to regulatory documents, the company's troubles began in February 2020 when its board voted to remove Sean Wyatt Mowray as an officer and director. While the Nevada Secretary of State received notification of these changes, the Gaming Control Board did not.

The situation escalated in July 2020 when Mowray transferred his 25% ownership stake to the Lusichs in exchange for a $25,000 credit against debts owed to the Lusich Family Trust. A few months later, in December 2020, another shareholder, Judith Elaine Hott, sold her 25% interest to the Lusichs for $20,000.

Both transfers violated Nevada gaming regulations because they occurred without prior approval from the Gaming Commission. State law requires advance authorization for any transfer of interest in a gaming license holder.

The complaint's third count focuses on false statements made in mandatory NGC-09 forms filed in March 2021 and March 2022. The company certified under penalty of perjury Mowray and Hott remained 25% owners and officers, despite their earlier departures. The forms also failed to disclose Diane Lusich's new positions as Secretary and Treasurer.

Regulators emphasized the particular gravity of these violations, noting ownership and officer positions constitute material facts in gaming license oversight. The company never attempted to correct these misstatements, despite filing accurate information about the transfers in separate documentation.

The Gaming Control Board seeks monetary fines for each violation and potential action against the company's gaming licenses. The case highlights Nevada's strict regulatory framework designed to maintain public confidence in the gaming industry through careful oversight of ownership changes and accurate reporting requirements.

Leid's Inc. Failed to Report Death

A Nevada Gaming Control Board complaint filed against Leid's Incorporated and its officers reveals multiple violations stemming from unreported shareholder death and unauthorized stock transactions.

The complaint, filed on September 1, 2023, centers on Leid's Incorporated, which operates P & L Launderland and Washtubs Coin-Laundry in Carson City. The company, along with Kevin Michael Leid and Janet Arleen Wells, faces disciplinary action for three distinct violations.

The first violation occurred when the company failed to notify the Gaming Control Board about the death of shareholder David Meril Leid on October 30, 2020. The board wasn't informed until October 28, 2021 - nearly a year after his death. Nevada gaming regulations require immediate notification of shareholder deaths.

The second count involves an unauthorized stock repurchase agreement. On July 2, 2021, Leid's Incorporated agreed to repurchase shares from Janet Wells in exchange for debt forgiveness worth $68,617.14. A subsequent agreement on October 20, 2021, corrected the number of shares from two to four. The company made these arrangements without prior Commission approval, violating state gaming regulations.

The third violation stems from another stock repurchase agreement made on October 20, 2021. The company agreed to buy Wells' remaining 28 shares plus 60 additional shares she expected to receive from David Leid's estate. Monthly payments of $5,529.51 began on November 1, 2021, before Commission approval.

When gaming officials notified the company on January 6, 2023, about the requirement to place payments in escrow, Leid's continued direct payments to Wells. The company's legal counsel acknowledged the risk but continued payments to maintain "peace in the valley."

By February 2023, Wells had received an estimated $88,472.16 in unauthorized payments. Though the Commission ultimately approved the stock disposition on February 23, 2023, the prior unauthorized transactions violated gaming regulations.

The Gaming Control Board seeks monetary fines and potential action against the company's gaming licenses. The case highlights Nevada's strict oversight of gaming-related business transactions and ownership changes.

River Plate's La Jolla Location - Entertainment Tax

The Nevada Gaming Control Board filed a complaint against River Plate, Inc., operating as La Jolla, for numerous violations related to live entertainment tax requirements spanning July 2019 through September 2021.

The Las Vegas establishment, located at 2245 East Flamingo Road, failed to maintain proper records and comply with internal control procedures despite previous warnings from the Gaming Control Board.

According to the complaint, River Plate neglected to keep essential documentation, including "Z-Tapes" and "Cashier Close-Out" reports for admission sales from May 2020 through September 2021. The company also failed to maintain accounting records verifying entertainment revenue during the review period.

The violations extended to the company's handling of complimentary admissions. While La Jolla offered free entry to military personnel and others on a discretionary basis, it did not record these transactions properly or maintain documentary evidence to support the deductions from entertainment revenue.

The Gaming Board's investigation revealed a pattern of recurring violations. The establishment had received violation letters in October 2017 and March 2020 for similar issues. Despite responding to these earlier notices with promises of correction, the problems persisted.

Other violations included:
- Failure to perform cash count reconciliations
- No documentation of investigations into large variances
- Lack of proper classification of gross sales into taxable and non-taxable components
- Missing cash register tapes for admission sales
- No monthly monitoring of entertainment sales accuracy
- Failure to post entertainment transactions to accounting records

The Board sent a violation letter to River Plate in April 2022, but the company did not respond. A subsequent Order to Show Cause in June 2022 received an inadequate response from the establishment.

The Gaming Control Board is seeking monetary fines and potential action against River Plate's gaming licenses and registrations. The case highlights the strict regulatory requirements for gaming establishments offering live entertainment in Nevada and the serious consequences of repeated non-compliance.

The Timbers Owner Gaming Violations in Carson City

The Nevada Gaming Control Board filed a complaint against Bette M. Larsen, owner of The Timbers bar in Carson City, alleging multiple violations of gaming regulations during the COVID-19 pandemic and operational irregularities.

During a May 5, 2021 inspection, gaming agents found approximately 20-30 patrons and three employees not wearing face coverings inside the establishment. The patrons were also not practicing social distancing as required by state directives. When an agent began taking photos, one employee quickly covered their face.

The violations came after a previous complaint in October 2020, where Larsen admitted similar COVID-19 safety violations and agreed to pay a $5,000 fine. As part of this settlement, she was required to file a key employee application by January 18, 2021 - a condition she failed to meet.

Further investigation revealed Larsen had transferred her gaming operation to The Timbers, LLC sometime after February 2007 without obtaining required Gaming Commission approval. Despite this transfer, she continued submitting annual attestations from 2018 through 2021 stating she remained the 100% owner of the operation.

The complaint also cites changes in property ownership. In 2007, Larsen and Michael Van Overbeke purchased the premises, and in March 2021, ownership transferred to Timbers Land, LLC. The

Gaming Board was never notified of these changes as required by regulations.

The Board's complaint outlines five counts against Larsen:
- Failure to enforce COVID-19 safety measures
- Non-compliance with license conditions regarding key employee applications
- Unauthorized transfer of gaming operations
- Filing false attestations about ownership
- Failure to report changes in property ownership

The Gaming Control Board seeks monetary fines for each violation and potential action against Larsen's gaming license. The case highlights the regulatory challenges faced by gaming establishments during the pandemic and the importance of maintaining accurate ownership records with gaming authorities.

Country Club Auto Spa - Drug Sales Discovery

The Nevada Gaming Control Board filed a complaint against LV Station Management Inc., doing business as Country Club Auto Spa, and its owner Ali Pourdastan, following the discovery of illegal drug sales and multiple violations at their Las Vegas location.

The investigation began when Las Vegas Metropolitan Police Department received an anonymous tip in March 2020 about narcotic activity at the convenience store licensed for five slot machines. Undercover officers made multiple drug purchases from an employee before executing a search warrant on December 17, 2020.

During the raid, police found a stolen handgun, ammunition, a small scale, and illegal narcotics. The employee admitted to selling approximately $200 worth of methamphetamine during work shifts.

Two other employees were also arrested - one for outstanding warrants and another discovered living in poor conditions in the building's attic.

The Gaming Control Board's complaint outlined six counts of violations, including failure to maintain proper control over business operations, endangering public safety, and non-compliance with license conditions.

The facility's key employee requirements went unfulfilled since December 2018. Three different key employees cycled through positions without proper applications being filed within the mandated 60-day window. The business also failed to maintain required employee lists and ensure staff had proper alcohol awareness certification cards.

Clark County authorities suspended Country Club Auto Spa's business and liquor licenses immediately following the police raid. While the company later received permission to resume operations under strict conditions, including hiring armed security and maintaining proper employee documentation, its gaming operations remained suspended except for one day of operation to preserve its license status.

The Gaming Commission can impose fines up to $100,000 for initial violations and $250,000 for subsequent violations. The Commission may also limit, condition, suspend or revoke gaming licenses as disciplinary action.

The case highlights Nevada's strict gaming regulations requiring licensees to maintain suitable operations protecting public safety and the industry's reputation. The Commission emphasizes gaming establishments must exercise proper control over their premises and comply with all state and local laws to retain their licenses.

Mohegan Sun Casino Las Vegas - Grand Opening

The Nevada Gaming Control Board filed a complaint against MGNV, LLC (Mohegan Sun Casino Las Vegas) for multiple violations of COVID-19 health and safety protocols during its March 25, 2021 opening at Virgin Hotels Las Vegas.

The violations came to light through photographs published in the Las Vegas Review-Journal and posts on Virgin Hotels Las Vegas' official Twitter account, showing numerous instances of non-compliance with state-mandated face covering requirements and social distancing guidelines.

In the first documented violation, photographs showed two patrons playing blackjack without face coverings while a third maskless patron stood closely behind them. None of the individuals were eating, drinking, or smoking – activities which would have permitted temporary mask removal.

A second violation involved at least five unmasked patrons seated in the Desert Star bar's lounge area without proper social distancing. The Review-Journal identified the patrons as Jackie Wiatrowski, April Swartz, Chelsea Dawn and Natalee Krista.

The third count stemmed from photographs showing large crowds of patrons failing to maintain proper social distancing while moving through the casino floor during the opening event.

In a high-profile fourth violation, television personality Mario Lopez was photographed throwing dice at a craps table without a face covering. Surveillance footage revealed Lopez remained maskless for approximately 10 minutes while taking photos with other patrons, drawing a crowd in violation of social distancing requirements.

The fifth count cited two additional Twitter photos posted by Virgin Hotels Las Vegas: one showing two maskless patrons at a slot machine, and another depicting a patron without a face covering blowing on dice at a craps table. The casino later removed these photos from their Twitter account.

The Nevada Occupational Safety & Health Administration had previously cited the casino on April 27, 2021, for failing to maintain social distancing between employees and guests, and for guests not wearing face coverings while within six feet of each other at table games.

The Gaming Control Board's complaint asks the Nevada Gaming Commission to impose monetary fines and take action against the casino's licenses for these violations of state gaming regulations and COVID-19 emergency directives.

Timbers Bar Owner - Protocol Failures

The Nevada Gaming Control Board filed a complaint against Bette M. Larsen, owner of The Timbers bar in Carson City, alleging multiple violations of COVID-19 safety protocols during an August 2020 inspection.

The case emerged after the Board received an anonymous complaint on August 17, 2020, reporting patrons at The Timbers were not wearing face coverings, the bar was overcrowded, and customers were not maintaining social distancing requirements.

During an inspection on August 26 at approximately 8:00 p.m., Board agents discovered all nine patrons and the bartender without face coverings. The agents observed customers clustered together at the bar front, violating social distancing guidelines.

When agents spoke with the bartender about the requirements, she acknowledged the face covering mandate and showed them her mask. However, she continued working without wearing it. The agents contacted Larsen to inform her of the violations.

The complaint alleges Larsen failed to comply with Governor Sisolak's Emergency Directives and the Board's Updated Health and Safety Policies for Reopening after Temporary Closure. These policies were implemented following the governor's March 12, 2020 Declaration of Emergency for COVID-19 and subsequent directives requiring face coverings and social distancing in public spaces.

The violations constitute an unsuitable method of operation under Nevada Gaming Commission Regulations 5.011, 5.011(a), 5.011(h), and 5.011(k). The Board seeks monetary fines and potential action against Larsen's gaming licenses.

The case highlights the Gaming Control Board's efforts to enforce COVID-19 safety measures within Nevada's gaming establishments during the pandemic. Under state regulations, licensees must maintain suitable methods of operation to protect public health, safety, and welfare.

SSM Gaming, LLC Gaming - Employee Registration

The Nevada Gaming Control Board filed a complaint against SSM Gaming, LLC for multiple violations related to expired gaming employee registrations and reporting failures. The case highlights ongoing compliance issues dating back to 2014.

In July 2014, SSM Gaming received a violation letter concerning four unregistered gaming employees. The employees - Barbara Thibodeau, Samuel Escobido, Mary Ann Matej, and Robert Nelson -

had worked without proper registration for periods ranging from one year and nine months to nearly twelve years.

The current complaint outlines five counts of violations occurring between 2019 and 2020. In Count One, Barbara Thibodeau, an accounting person, worked with an expired gaming registration from July 14, 2019, until May 14, 2020. She continued her duties through Nevada's gaming shutdown on March 17, 2020.

Count Two involves Samuel Escobido, a slot machine mechanic, whose registration expired July 14, 2019. He worked approximately eight months with an expired registration until March 17, 2020. His registration was renewed May 14, 2020.

In Count Three, Mary Ann Matej, another slot machine mechanic, worked eight months with an expired registration from July 14, 2019, through March 17, 2020. Like her colleagues, her registration was renewed May 14, 2020.

Count Four details Robert Nelson's case, a slot machine mechanic whose registration expired July 14, 2019. He continued working for eight months without valid registration until his termination March 18, 2020.

The final count addresses SSM Gaming's failure to report Nelson's termination. The company missed the April 15, 2020 deadline to enter his termination date into the Board's online system, waiting until May 8, 2020, to update the records.

The Gaming Control Board seeks monetary fines and potential action against SSM Gaming's licenses for these violations, citing them as unsuitable methods of operation under Nevada gaming regulations.

Kopper Keg South Faces Gaming Violations - Pandemic

The Nevada Gaming Control Board filed a complaint against Kopper Keg South on August 13, 2020, alleging violations of gaming regulations during COVID-19 restrictions.

The case stems from observations made by a Gaming Control Board agent on July 31, 2020, at approximately 9:30 p.m. The agent discovered six patrons playing bar top slot machines at the establishment, located at 2375 East Torino Avenue in Las Vegas. According to the complaint, these machines were operational and available for patron use, despite emergency directives prohibiting such activity.

The violations occurred against the backdrop of Nevada Governor Steve Sisolak's series of emergency declarations and directives responding to the COVID-19 pandemic. On March 12, 2020, Sisolak declared a state of emergency, followed by a March 17 mandate shutting down all gaming machines and related equipment. Subsequent directives established phased reopening plans with specific restrictions.

Critical to this case, Directive 027, issued July 10, 2020, required bar tops and bar areas in counties with elevated disease transmission to remain closed to customers. Clark County, where Kopper Keg South operates, fell under this designation.

The Gaming Control Board charged Kopper Keg South with violating Nevada Gaming Commission Regulation 5.011, which considers any activity inimical to public health, safety, morals, good order, or general welfare as an unsuitable method of operation.

The Board seeks monetary fines and potential action against Kopper Keg South's gaming licenses. The complaint emphasizes the gaming industry's responsibility to maintain public confidence and trust through strict regulation and compliance with state laws and emergency directives.

Grand Sierra Resort - 19 Safety Violations

The Nevada Gaming Control Board filed a complaint against MEI-GSR Holdings LLC, operating as Grand Sierra Resort and Casino (GSR) in Reno, for repeatedly failing to enforce COVID-19 safety protocols during summer 2020.

Board agents documented three separate incidents where GSR staff failed to ensure patrons wore face coverings and maintained social distancing requirements mandated by Nevada Governor Steve Sisolak's emergency directives.

On June 19, agents observed two patrons gambling at separate table games without face coverings, while GSR employees made no attempts to enforce the mask requirement. The operations manager said he would remind table games staff about face covering rules after being notified.

The violations escalated on July 2, when agents found at least 43 patrons in gaming areas either not wearing masks or wearing them improperly. Three GSR employees walked past non-compliant patrons without addressing the violations. The casino shift manager immediately addressed the issue with staff after being informed.

The most extensive violations occurred on July 31, when agents documented 34 patrons without proper face coverings, including four who interacted directly with GSR employees who failed to enforce the mandate. Additionally, approximately 50 patrons queued for hotel elevators without maintaining required social distancing, with no staff present to manage the crowding.

During the same July visit, agents observed a GSR marketing promotion where the host failed to wear a face covering properly while addressing a crowd of at least 22 patrons who were not socially distanced. Staff only addressed these violations after being notified by Board agents.

The complaint cites three counts of violations against GSR for failing to meet gaming license standards and operating unsuitably under Nevada Gaming Commission regulations. Each count alleges GSR failed to protect public health and safety, exercise sound judgment, comply with state laws, and maintain proper operational standards.

The Gaming Control Board seeks monetary fines for each separate violation and potential action against GSR's gaming licenses. The case will be heard by the Nevada Gaming Commission for disciplinary proceedings.

The violations occurred despite clear emergency directives requiring gaming establishments to ensure patron compliance with face covering requirements and social distancing guidelines as conditions for reopening after the state's mandatory gaming shutdown in March 2020.

Sahara Las Vegas - Protocol Breaches

The Nevada Gaming Control Board filed a complaint against SB Gaming LLC, operating as Sahara Las Vegas, for multiple violations of COVID-19 health and safety protocols during summer 2020.

In early June 2020, the Board received an anonymous tip alleging Sahara employees allowed more players in the slot area than permitted under COVID-19 safety guidelines. A subsequent covert investigation on June 16 revealed three separate violations.

An agent observed four patrons at a craps table when only three were actively playing, violating requirements for social distancing and betting station separation. At a blackjack table, a non-playing patron stood between two active players, breaching similar distancing protocols. The agent also witnessed five individuals gathering around a single slot machine player, contradicting rules prohibiting group congregation.

The Assistant Casino Manager acknowledged and corrected the table game violations immediately when notified. The slot machine group had dispersed before intervention was needed. The Board issued a violation letter to Sahara on June 18.

A more serious breach occurred on July 23, when Sahara hosted a local trade organization luncheon attended by approximately 135 people in its Congo Conference Rooms. This violated Governor Steve Sisolak's Emergency Directive 021, limiting gatherings to 50 or fewer individuals.

When questioned, Sahara's Vice President of Hotel Sales claimed he received approval from the Chief Financial Officer and Vice President of Government Affairs, who allegedly had verbal authorization from a Board member. The VP of Government Affairs later admitted a "misunderstanding" about occupancy limits, believing food and beverage events could operate at 50% restaurant capacity.

The complaint outlines two counts against Sahara. Count I addresses the conference room gathering violation, while Count II encompasses the three gaming floor social distancing breaches. Both counts cite failures to meet gaming license standards and maintain proper operations under Nevada Gaming Commission regulations.

The Board seeks monetary fines and potential action against Sahara's gaming licenses. The case highlights Nevada gaming regulators' efforts to enforce COVID-19 safety measures in the state's casinos during the pandemic.

United Coin Machine - Bar-Top Slots During Pandemic

A Nevada Gaming Control Board agent discovered six active bar-top slot machines at Cheers in Winnemucca on July 16, 2020, leading to a complaint against United Coin Machine Co., doing business as Century Gaming Technologies.

The violation occurred during heightened COVID-19 restrictions in Humboldt County, which had been designated an area with Elevated Disease Transmission. Under Governor Steve Sisolak's Emergency Directive 027, issued July 10, 2020, bar tops and bar areas in counties with elevated transmission rates were required to close to customers.

During the agent's 6:00 p.m. inspection, they observed a patron actively playing one of the six available bar-top machines. The agent immediately reported the violation to the business operator, who covered the slot machines to prevent further patron access. United Coin Machine shut off the machines the following day at approximately 11:30 a.m.

The complaint alleges United Coin Machine violated Nevada Gaming Commission Regulation 5.011, constituting an unsuitable method of operation. The regulation requires gaming establishments to comply with all federal, state, and local laws while maintaining proper standards of custom and decorum.

The Gaming Control Board seeks monetary fines and potential action against United Coin Machine's licenses. The case highlights

Nevada's strict enforcement of COVID-19 safety measures in gaming establishments during the pandemic, particularly in areas with elevated transmission rates.

The incident occurred amid a series of emergency directives issued by Governor Sisolak to control the spread of COVID-19, beginning with his March 12, 2020 Declaration of Emergency and subsequent orders limiting gaming operations throughout the state.

Three Nevada Casinos - Mask Violations

In a complaint filed August 31, 2020, the Nevada Gaming Control Board brought disciplinary action against three affiliated casinos - COD Casino, Cactus Jack's Senator Club, and Jackpot Crossing Casino - for repeatedly failing to enforce face covering requirements during the COVID-19 pandemic.

The case emerged after an anonymous complaint on July 15, 2020, alleged COD Casino management wasn't enforcing mask requirements in its smoking section. A Gaming Board agent met with the Vice President of Operations (VPO), who oversees all three properties, to discuss the complaint. According to the filing, the VPO appeared "upset, dismissive and defiant" and insisted on seeing written orders about mask requirements for smoking and drinking patrons.

During the inspection, the agent observed six patrons either not wearing masks or wearing them improperly. When informed, the VPO claimed one patron had health issues but provided no explanation for the other violations.

A follow-up inspection on July 20 revealed more violations at COD Casino, with three employees - including managers - improperly wearing masks while interacting with each other. Agents also found multiple patrons without proper face coverings.

The problems extended to the other properties. At Cactus Jack's, an inspection on July 21 found five out of twelve patrons and a bartender violating mask protocols. A shift manager told agents some customers had medical exemptions or "specific permission" from management to forgo masks.

The same day at Jackpot Crossing, agents documented nine patrons wearing masks incorrectly and observed two managers speaking together with their masks pulled down to their chins.

The Gaming Board filed four separate counts against the properties for violating Nevada Gaming Commission regulations. The violations occurred despite multiple reminders about mask requirements and over a month after the Board mandated proper PPE use by employees.

All three casinos are indirectly owned by David Scott Tate and share the same VPO. The complaint seeks monetary fines and potential action against the properties' gaming licenses.

The case highlights Nevada gaming regulators' efforts to enforce COVID-19 safety measures, which Governor Steve Sisolak implemented through emergency directives requiring face coverings for both casino employees and patrons to help contain the spreading pandemic.

Hotel Nevada & Gambling Hall - Violations

The Nevada Gaming Control Board filed a complaint against Hotel Nevada & Gambling Hall in Ely for multiple violations of COVID-19 safety protocols during July 2020.

According to the complaint, gaming board agents conducted three separate inspections at the establishment, revealing consistent failures to enforce face covering requirements for both employees and patrons.

During the first inspection on July 17, agents observed three employees either not wearing face coverings or wearing them improperly. The violations were discussed with the manager and general manager on site. On the same day, agents noted three patrons also failed to comply with face covering mandates, with no intervention from hotel staff.

In a follow-up inspection on July 22, the situation had not improved. Agents photographed at least four patrons without proper face coverings. Staff only moved to address these violations when they noticed agents taking photographs.

The violations occurred despite Governor Steve Sisolak's emergency directives requiring face coverings in public spaces and the Gaming Control Board's updated health and safety policies. The governor's June 24 directive specifically mandated businesses to ensure all patrons wear face coverings and authorized the Gaming Control Board to pursue disciplinary action against non-compliant licensees.

The complaint cites three counts of violating Nevada Gaming Commission Regulation 5.011, deeming the hotel's actions "unsuitable methods of operation." Each count represents a separate inspection where violations were documented.

The Gaming Control Board seeks monetary fines for each violation and possible action against the hotel's gaming licenses. The case highlights Nevada gaming regulators' efforts to enforce COVID-19 safety measures in the state's gaming establishments during the pandemic.

The hotel, located at 501 Aultman Street in Ely, holds a nonrestricted gaming license and bears responsibility for complying with all Nevada Gaming Control Act provisions and Commission regulations.

Waldman Investments - Restrictions

The Nevada Gaming Control Board filed a complaint against Waldman Investments, Inc., operating as Bowl Incline in Incline Village, for allegedly violating gaming regulations during the COVID-19 pandemic.

The case stems from observations made on July 11, 2020, when a Gaming Board agent visited the establishment at approximately 5:30 p.m. The agent discovered bar top slot machines remained in service and available for patron play, with chairs positioned in front of every other slot machine.

This arrangement violated Governor Steve Sisolak's Emergency Directive 027, issued on July 10, 2020. The directive mandated bar tops and bar areas in counties with Elevated Disease Transmission must close to customers. At the time, Washoe County, where Bowl Incline operates, was designated as having Elevated Disease Transmission according to Department of Health and Human Services criteria.

The violation came after months of evolving COVID-19 restrictions. On March 12, 2020, Governor Sisolak declared a state of emergency, followed by a March 17 mandate to shut down all gaming machines. Through subsequent directives, gaming operations remained closed until June 4, 2020, when a phased reopening began under strict Gaming Control Board requirements.

The Board's complaint cites Bowl Incline for violating Nevada Gaming Commission Regulation 5.011, constituting an unsuitable method of operation. The Board seeks monetary fines and potential action against Bowl Incline's gaming licenses.

The case highlights the Gaming Control Board's role in enforcing COVID-19 safety measures within Nevada's gaming industry during the pandemic. The Board maintains these regulations protect public health while preserving the gaming industry's reputation and the state's economic interests.

Fremont Hotel and Casino - Wrongful Detention

The Nevada Gaming Control Board filed a complaint against Sam-Will, Inc., operating as Fremont Hotel and Casino, following a serious incident involving the wrongful detention and coerced payment from an innocent casino patron.

On November 24, 2019, security personnel at Fremont wrongfully detained a female patron after another guest accused her of stealing slot machine credits. The detained patron had legitimately won money playing slots when security officers suddenly grabbed her from behind, handcuffed her, and marched her across the casino floor.

During her 90-minute detention, security staff berated the woman, ignored her protests of innocence, and failed to properly investigate readily available evidence which would have proven her innocence. Surveillance footage and slot machine records clearly showed she had not stolen any credits.

The complaint outlines four major violations by Fremont:

Count I alleges the casino failed to exercise sound judgment by not conducting a proper investigation, leading to wrongful detention and coerced payment through threats of imprisonment.

Count II focuses on excessive force used during the detention. Security officers violated the casino's own procedures by failing to give verbal commands before physical contact and using unnecessary restraints on a non-threatening individual.

Count III charges Fremont with providing inaccurate and incomplete information to Las Vegas Metropolitan Police Department officers and Gaming Control Board agents, hampering their investigations.

Count IV addresses Fremont's inadequate response during the subsequent investigation, including missing crucial information and inconsistent statements.

The Board found Fremont's actions particularly egregious as basic slot machine records would have immediately shown the detained patron's innocence. Instead, she was held in handcuffs, intimidated into paying $202 she didn't owe, and banned from the property.

The complaint seeks monetary fines and potential action against Fremont's gaming license. Under Nevada law, each violation could result in fines up to $100,000 for initial complaints and $250,000 for subsequent violations.

This case highlights the Gaming Control Board's commitment to protecting casino patrons and maintaining proper operational standards in Nevada's gaming industry. The Board emphasized how Fremont's actions reflected poorly on Nevada's gaming industry and violated multiple regulations regarding suitable operations.

Stateside Lounge - Gang-Related Homicide

The Nevada Gaming Control Board filed a complaint against Fabes, LLC, operating as Stateside Lounge, and its owner Luca Fabian Bartolini following escalating gang activity and a fatal shooting at the Las Vegas establishment.

Between January 2018 and June 2019, Las Vegas Metropolitan Police Department (LVMPD) responded to 72 calls at Stateside Lounge, including nine violent crimes and three property crimes. The venue became a significant drain on police resources as it emerged as the most problematic location within LVMPD's Downtown Area Command.

The situation culminated in a homicide on June 22, 2019, when a gang-related altercation inside the bar spilled outside, resulting in 30-40 rounds of gunfire and one death. Neither Bartolini nor his staff called 911 to report the shooting.

During the homicide investigation, Bartolini initially lied to police, claiming the shooting had no connection to his bar and he wasn't present. He later admitted being on-site but insisted he didn't hear the altercation from his office behind the bar. When asked about surveillance footage, Bartolini claimed a power surge had destroyed the DVR system days earlier.

The complaint outlined three major counts against Stateside Lounge and Bartolini:

Count I alleged violations of state gaming regulations for failing to maintain proper control over business operations and allowing dangerous conditions to persist. The establishment catered to gang members and ignored LVMPD's security recommendations.

Count II focused on Bartolini's dishonesty during the homicide investigation, demonstrating a lack of suitable character for gaming licensure.

Count III cited violations of Las Vegas Municipal Code for employing security personnel without proper work cards and failing to maintain required employee documentation.

Prior to these incidents, LVMPD had repeatedly warned Bartolini about gang activity at his establishment. Despite police intervention, he failed to implement recommended security measures such as hiring professional security, installing metal detectors, or searching patrons' bags.

The landlord had also cautioned Bartolini about the changing clientele and advised hiring security, but these warnings went unheeded. Following the homicide, the City of Las Vegas temporarily suspended Stateside's business license until July 8, 2019.

Bartolini ultimately chose to surrender the property to his landlord and attempted to voluntarily surrender his gaming license. The Gaming Control Board responded by placing administrative holds on both Bartolini's and Stateside's licenses pending disciplinary action.

Five-Count Complaint Against Stephen Wynn

The Nevada Gaming Control Board filed a complaint seeking to revoke former casino mogul Stephen Wynn's gaming license, citing multiple instances of sexual misconduct with subordinate employees and his failure to appear at an investigative hearing.

The complaint outlines five counts against Wynn, who served as CEO and Chairman of Wynn Resorts until his resignation in 2018. According to the filing, multiple women in subordinate positions reported unwanted sexual advances from Wynn, who allegedly concealed the allegations through private settlements and nondisclosure agreements.

In Count One, investigators found evidence of sexual conduct between Wynn and subordinate employees, with victims describing feeling powerless due to their financial dependence on continued employment. The Board stated Wynn's behavior was "not consistent with good character" and posed a threat to Nevada's public interest.

Count Two focuses on Wynn's violation of company policies requiring professional workplace conduct. The company admitted in a 2019 settlement Wynn's actions were "inappropriate and unsuitable" given his position of power over employees.

Counts Three and Four detail specific incidents involving two employees. In 2005, a manicurist alleged sexual assault by Wynn resulting in pregnancy, leading to a $7.5 million private settlement. In 2006, a cocktail server reported sexual assault, resulting in a $975,000 settlement. Both agreements included strict confidentiality requirements.

Count Five addresses Wynn's failure to appear at a September 7, 2018 investigative hearing despite receiving proper notice. The Board emphasized this refusal hindered their investigation and constitutes grounds for license revocation.

The Board seeks monetary fines for each violation and revocation of Wynn's gaming license. Earlier settlements with Wynn Resorts resulted in a $20 million fine from Nevada regulators and $35 million from Massachusetts gaming authorities.

The complaint details a "systemic failure" and "pervasive culture of non-disclosure" at Wynn Resorts during Wynn's tenure, resulting in worldwide negative publicity and damage to Nevada's gaming industry reputation.

Matthew Maddox, who succeeded Wynn as CEO, testified before Massachusetts regulators "there were many victims, and those victims felt powerless." The company acknowledged its failure to investigate sexual harassment allegations and properly address complaints against its former chairman.

Smuggle Inn - Cocaine Sales by Employees

The Nevada Gaming Control Board filed a complaint against Smuggle Inn, a restricted gaming license holder located at 1305A Vegas Valley Drive in Las Vegas, following multiple incidents of cocaine sales by employees in December 2018.

According to the complaint, Las Vegas Metropolitan Police Department detectives discovered several Smuggle Inn employees selling cocaine to patrons on December 9, 2018. An undercover operation revealed a bartender selling cocaine from behind the bar while on duty. A warrant remains active for this employee's arrest as of May 1, 2019.

A second incident occurred on December 17, 2018, when another bartender sold cocaine to undercover detectives, again conducting the transaction from behind the bar during their shift.

The situation escalated on December 26, 2018, when Metro police executed a search warrant at the establishment. Officers found the lone bartender on duty in possession of 69.3 grams of cocaine, 5.7 grams of methamphetamine, and $6,222 in cash. This employee later pleaded guilty to Possession of a Controlled Substance with

Intent to Sell, a Category D Felony, with sentencing scheduled for May 30, 2019.

Following the search warrant execution, Metro cited Smuggle Inn for allowing narcotic sales inside its business and issued an emergency suspension.

The Gaming Control Board's complaint alleges Smuggle Inn failed to prevent these activities, violating Nevada gaming regulations requiring establishments to operate in a manner suitable to protect public health, safety, morals, and welfare. The Board argues these incidents reflect poorly on Nevada's gaming industry and constitute an unsuitable method of operation.

The complaint seeks monetary penalties for each violation and potential action against Smuggle Inn's gaming license. Under Nevada law, gaming licenses are considered revocable privileges, with licensees required to maintain strict compliance with state regulations and demonstrate ongoing suitability to hold a license.

Wynn Resorts - Sexual Misconduct Claims

The Nevada Gaming Control Board launched an extensive investigation into Wynn Las Vegas and Wynn Resorts following a January 2018 Wall Street Journal article exposing allegations of sexual misconduct by former CEO Steve Wynn.

Through interviews and document reviews, investigators uncovered multiple instances where executives failed to properly investigate sexual harassment claims against Wynn spanning over a decade.

In 2005, a Wynn salon employee alleged she was raped by Wynn and became pregnant. Though salon management reported it to HR, senior executives including the president, VP of hotel operations, and HR chief never initiated an investigation. Wynn later paid the employee $7.5 million in a private settlement.

A year later, a cocktail server alleged Wynn pressured her into a nonconsensual sexual relationship lasting from 2005-2006. She received a $975,000 settlement, but again, no investigation was conducted by executives aware of the claims.

The pattern continued in 2014 when three Encore spa employees reported sexual harassment during massages performed on Wynn. Despite multiple managers learning of the allegations, none ensured proper reporting to employee relations for investigation as required by company policy.

In 2016, a flight attendant sent written complaints about Wynn harassing multiple attendants. Two top legal executives received the correspondence but failed to initiate required investigations.

The complaint also cites failures to investigate rumors a manager was facilitating sexual relationships between cocktail servers and Wynn or guests, and allegations about another executive "loving to sleep with cocktail servers."

Wynn Resorts maintained policies requiring sexual harassment investigations and discouraging relationships between supervisors and employees. However, the board found these policies were not consistently enforced, especially regarding executives. Wynn himself never attended required compliance training and spa policies did not apply to him.

The gaming board is seeking fines and potential action against Wynn Resorts' gaming licenses for what it calls "unsuitable methods of operation" and failures to protect employees. The complaint alleges the company's actions damaged Nevada gaming's reputation and failed to maintain required high standards of operation.

Wynn resigned from all positions in February 2018 and divested his ownership interests by March 2018. The gaming commission has placed administrative holds on all his gaming approvals.

Former Pit Supervisor - $50K Points Scheme

A former pit supervisor at The Cosmopolitan of Las Vegas orchestrated a three-year fraudulent player tracking scheme, resulting in approximately $50,000 in illegitimate points for his wife, according to a Nevada Gaming Control Board complaint.

Gregory Walter Norris, who worked as a pit supervisor at The Cosmopolitan from May 2013 to February 2017, came under investigation after suspicious activities were noticed involving him and his wife, Jacqueline Iannotti, later identified as Jacqueline Norris.

The casino's investigation uncovered Norris had been creating false ratings for his wife in the player tracking system by using another pit supervisor's login credentials. His wife never actually engaged in any gaming activity during the periods when Norris entered the fraudulent ratings.

The scheme involved manipulating the player tracking system by inputting false data about patron gaming activity, including buy-ins, average bets, and losses. These ratings generated points his wife could redeem for various casino perks.

Of the $50,000 worth of illegitimate points accumulated, Mrs. Norris redeemed approximately $17,000 in complimentary services, including food and beverages, hotel room nights, and free promotional gaming chips.

Gaming Control Board agents responded to The Cosmopolitan on January 19, 2017, after being informed of the internal investigation findings. Criminal charges followed on May 22, 2017, leading to Norris pleading guilty to Conspiracy to Commit a Crime - Theft, a gross misdemeanor, on April 10, 2018.

At the time of the complaint, Norris was employed as a Table Games Supervisor at the Tropicana Las Vegas. The Nevada Gaming Control Board seeks to revoke his gaming employee registration, citing violations under NRS 463.337, which allows for revocation if an employee commits larceny or embezzlement against a gaming licensee or is convicted of a gross misdemeanor.

Best Bet Products - Surveillance Plans

The Nevada Gaming Control Board filed a complaint against Best Bet Products Inc., operating as Stagestop Casino in Pahrump, and its president Shawn Paul Holmes for repeatedly failing to submit required surveillance plans and ignoring multiple requests from gaming regulators.

According to the complaint filed on April 12, 2018, Stagestop Casino neglected to file mandatory annual surveillance plan reports for 2016 and 2017. The casino also failed to submit surveillance plans for all previous years it operated gaming activities.

Nevada gaming regulations require casinos to provide yearly updates about changes to their surveillance systems or confirm no modifications were made. These reports help ensure gaming establishments maintain proper security oversight.

The complaint outlines a pattern of non-responsiveness by Holmes and Stagestop Casino. Board agents made numerous attempts throughout 2016 and 2017 to obtain the missing reports:

- Staff provided Holmes with template forms and reminders about filing requirements
- A January 2017 email inquiry went unanswered
- The casino ignored industry-wide notices about electronic filing procedures
- Holmes failed to return a December 2017 voicemail warning of potential disciplinary action
- A casino bartender promised to compile the report but never submitted it

By late December 2017, despite multiple conversations and assurances, Stagestop Casino had not produced any of the required surveillance documentation.

The Gaming Control Board charged the casino with violating regulations requiring compliance with state gaming laws and cooperation with gaming authorities. The complaint seeks monetary fines and potential action against Stagestop's gaming licenses.

The case highlights Nevada regulators' emphasis on maintaining strict oversight of casino surveillance systems as part of ensuring gaming integrity and public confidence in the industry.

Teresa Serrano - TITO Voucher Scheme

In a complaint filed April 10, 2018, the Nevada Gaming Control Board seeks to revoke the gaming registration of Teresa Serrano following her alleged involvement in a TITO voucher theft scheme at the Venetian Resort Hotel Casino.

According to the complaint, Serrano redeemed several TITO vouchers at a Venetian kiosk on December 25, 2017. The vouchers had been improperly obtained by her husband, Romeo Serrano, during his employment as a slot manager at the property.

The complaint details one specific incident where a slot machine entered tilt mode on December 14, 2017. After the patron received a hand pay, the machine was taken out of service. The following day, when a slot technician serviced the machine, they printed TITO voucher No. 611355 for $921.00 and handed it to Romeo Serrano. Instead of following Venetian policy to place it with voided tickets, Romeo Serrano pocketed the voucher.

When Teresa Serrano redeemed the vouchers on December 25, Venetian security detained her. Board agents responded and found two stacks of U.S. currency in her purse - $1,052.00 and $879.00 - matching the amounts of the redeemed vouchers.

During questioning, Serrano admitted her husband provided the vouchers and she knew he had found them on the Venetian gaming floor. Board agents arrested her on charges of theft and conspiracy to commit theft.

The case carries additional weight as Serrano worked as a cage cashier at the Hard Rock Hotel and Casino at the time of the incident. The Gaming Control Board cites NRS 463.337(2) in its complaint, which allows the Commission to revoke gaming employee registration for individuals who commit, attempt, or conspire to commit larceny against a gaming licensee or on licensed gaming premises.

The Board has requested the Nevada Gaming Commission serve Serrano with the complaint and proceed with revoking her gaming employee registration.

Skyline Casino Faces - Employee Registration Issues

The Nevada Gaming Control Board filed a complaint against Northumberland LMG Corporation, operating as Skyline Casino in Henderson, Nevada, for several violations related to employee registration and reporting requirements.

According to the complaint, Skyline Casino employed a security guard, David Phillips, with an expired gaming employee registration for approximately 14 months. Phillips worked from August 11, 2016, through October 27, 2017, without proper registration, violating state regulations. His registration was finally renewed on October 28, 2017.

The Board also cited the casino for failing to submit mandatory gaming employee hire reports from May 2016 through October 2016. While Skyline eventually submitted these reports on November 21, 2016, it continued to fall behind. The casino later submitted reports covering November 2016 through September 2017 on October 18, 2017. As of January 10, 2018, reports for October and November 2017 remained outstanding.

In a third violation, the Board discovered 19 separated gaming employees were not properly recorded in their online registration system. Some terminations dated back to September 2014, yet these employees remained listed as current workers in Board records. The casino failed to submit written reports about these separated employees as required.

The Board had attempted to address these issues through multiple communications, sending emails to Skyline Casino on August 16, 2016, November 20, 2016, May 29, 2017, and October 17, 2017. The Board's Employee Registration unit Program Manager even made direct contact with Skyline's General Manager by phone on October 17, 2017, regarding the missing hire reports.

The Gaming Control Board seeks monetary fines for each violation and potential action against Skyline Casino's gaming licenses. The complaint emphasizes these violations constitute unsuitable methods of operation under Nevada gaming regulations.

Golden Route - Verify Business Operators

In a complaint filed November 2017, the Nevada Gaming Control Board alleged Golden Route Operations and Sartini Gaming violated gaming regulations by failing to verify business operators and maintain proper procedures at a Reno establishment.

The case centers on Floyd's Fireside in Reno, where Golden Route Operations and Sartini Gaming continued operating slot machines after the primary business operator changed hands. According to the complaint, Thomas H. Floyd Enterprises sold the business to Colt Family LLC in June 2016, but the gaming companies kept their slots running despite the ownership transfer.

The Board highlighted how Golden Route Operations had previously settled a similar complaint in 2013. In the settlement, the company claimed it implemented procedures to verify business operators before installing gaming devices. However, when asked to provide these written procedures in March 2017, the company could only produce a checklist - raising questions about whether proper protocols existed.

The complaint outlines two major violations. In Count One, regulators allege the gaming companies should have known about the business operator change through public records and an assignment agreement they received. Even after being contacted by Gaming Board agents in December 2016 and January 2017 about the operator change, the companies continued running slots until February 8, 2017, when explicitly told to shut them down.

Count Two focuses on the companies' failure to maintain or demonstrate compliance with the verification procedures promised in their 2013 settlement. The Board found no evidence in company files showing they completed required verifications at Floyd's Fireside or other approved locations.

The Gaming Control Board seeks fines and potential action against the companies' gaming licenses. The case underscores Nevada regulators' emphasis on proper verification of business operators and maintaining suitable gaming operations.

The matter awaits action by the Nevada Gaming Commission, which has authority to impose fines and take disciplinary action against gaming licenses for violations of state gaming laws and regulations.

Gaming Laboratories International - Testing Case

The Nevada Gaming Control Board filed a complaint against Gaming Laboratories International, LLC (GLI) for failing to properly test a gaming system and breaching independence requirements while certifying casino equipment.

According to the complaint, GLI, a registered independent testing laboratory in Nevada, improperly certified Interblock d.d.'s Pulse Arena System in December 2016. The Pulse Arena System allows patrons to place wagers through terminals on slot games, automated table games, and live table games.

The system required integration with IGT Advantage cashless wagering and slot metering system for revenue reporting and cashless wagering functions. However, GLI certified the system without performing this crucial integration, instead relying on data and reports provided by Interblock.

The Board outlined three major violations:

In Count I, GLI failed to integrate the Pulse Arena System with IGT Advantage during testing, violating multiple Nevada Gaming Commission regulations. The laboratory's reliance on manufacturer-provided data compromised its independence and testing protocols.

Count II revealed GLI staff actively participated in designing and developing the system's components. Emails showed GLI managers and engineers helped create reports and calculations for Interblock, including revenue reports and table game statistics. This involvement violated regulations requiring testing laboratories to remain independent from manufacturers.

In Count III, the Board alleged GLI breached confidentiality by sharing sample reports and information from other manufacturers' certification processes with Interblock. The laboratory provided multiple confidential reports to Interblock in November 2016, including table games statistical analyses and voucher tracking reports.

The Gaming Control Board seeks monetary fines for each violation and potential action against GLI's laboratory registration. The complaint emphasized GLI's conduct risked public confidence in gaming, Nevada's reputation, and accurate revenue accounting.

The case highlights the strict regulatory requirements for independence and proper testing protocols in Nevada's gaming industry, where testing laboratories play a crucial role in maintaining gaming integrity.

Rebel Oil Company Faces - Improper Business Sale

The Nevada Gaming Control Board filed a complaint against Rebel Oil Company for multiple gaming violations across 12 locations after an investigation revealed unauthorized slot machine operations following a complex business sale transaction.

According to the complaint, Rebel Oil entered into an Asset Purchase and Sale Agreement with a third-party purchaser on June 8, 2015. The deal included selling multiple businesses, encompassing buildings, improvements, leasehold interests, trade names, and logos - but explicitly excluded gaming assets.

The transaction took an unusual turn when Rebel Oil simultaneously entered into two additional agreements on December 18, 2015. First, a Leaseback Agreement with the third-party landlord allowed Rebel Oil to lease back the 12 locations for $1.00 per month. Second, a Management Agreement gave a third-party manager complete control of the businesses' operations, including supervision, employee management, inventory, expenses, marketing, and taxes.

The Management Agreement specified the third-party manager would receive 100% of non-gaming receipts, while Rebel Oil retained gaming proceeds. However, this arrangement violated Nevada gaming regulations because Rebel Oil was no longer the primary business operator - a requirement for maintaining restricted gaming licenses.

The Gaming Control Board notified Rebel Oil's attorney on December 22, 2015, the company could not continue gaming operations unless the third-party manager filed a key employee application. Rebel Oil ignored this directive and continued operating slot machines at all locations.

The situation came to a head at a March 3, 2016, Board hearing where Rebel Oil agreed to temporarily shut down its slot machines. The company filed a key employee application the next day and immediately resumed gaming operations.

During the period of unauthorized operation from December 22, 2015, through March 3, 2016, Rebel Oil generated $416,158.85 in net gaming revenue and paid $281,285.61 to the third-party manager for machine placement.

The Board's complaint charges each of the 12 Rebel Oil locations with violating Nevada gaming laws and regulations by operating slot machines without proper authority. The Board seeks monetary fines and potential action against the companies' gaming licenses.

Scoundrels Pub - Multiple Gang Shootings

The Nevada Gaming Control Board filed a complaint against Scoundrels Pub and its owner David John Zderic, citing repeated gang violence and failure to maintain proper security measures at the Las Vegas establishment.

According to the complaint, Las Vegas Metropolitan Police Department (LVMPD) documented Scoundrels as a gang hangout since 2009, with six gang-related shooting events occurring inside or outside the premises. Police records show 144 calls for service between 2009 and 2015, with 97 labeled as violent incidents.

Three major shootings in 2015 escalated concerns. In January, an unknown subject fired nine bullets into the building from a vehicle. In April, employees spotted armed men loading weapons before shots were fired into the establishment. The most severe incident occurred in December when four shooters exchanged 60-70 rounds in the parking lot, resulting in three people being hospitalized with gunshot wounds.

The complaint alleges staff attempted to conceal evidence after the December shooting. Surveillance footage from an adjacent store showed an employee sweeping up shell casings before police arrived. Staff denied the incident and failed to call 911 or maintain required incident logs.

Clark County authorities had previously placed conditions on Scoundrels' liquor license, requiring updated employee lists, incident reporting, and security personnel. The pub repeatedly failed to meet these requirements, leading to the license's revocation in December 2015.

The Gaming Control Board's complaint outlines three counts against Scoundrels and Zderic:

Count I: Failure to exercise proper control over operations, creating dangerous conditions for public safety
Count II: Interference with police investigation and failure to report criminal activity
Count III: Non-compliance with Clark County Code and gaming regulations

The complaint seeks monetary fines and potential action against the gaming licenses of both Scoundrels and Zderic. The establishment ceased operations after a fire in late 2015 and has not resumed gaming activities.

The case highlights the Gaming Commission's emphasis on maintaining public safety and preventing criminal activity at licensed gaming establishments in Nevada.

Doc Holliday's Owner Faces Multiple Gaming Violations

The Nevada Gaming Control Board filed a complaint against Silverado Ranch Restaurants LLC (Doc Holliday's), Brewery Restaurants LLC (4 Play), and Thomas James Brletic for multiple violations of gaming regulations and statutes.

According to the complaint, Brletic engaged in unauthorized sale activities in May 2015 when he entered a verbal agreement to sell Doc Holliday's to Heidi and James Gray. The Grays paid $10,000 in cash outside of escrow toward the purchase, with two $5,000 payments made on May 30 and June 8, 2015. A written agreement for the sale was signed on June 8. The Grays paid over $30,000 in additional expenses before withdrawing from the purchase agreement by June 30, 2015.

The complaint alleges both establishments failed to maintain required key employee positions. Doc Holliday's operated without filing a key employee application from September 2014 to July 2015, after its previous key employee Robert James Phillips departed. Similarly, 4 Play failed to file any key employee application from its license activation in October 2014 through at least February 2016.

Further violations included unpaid gaming fees. Doc Holliday's continued operating through July 1, 2015, but failed to pay $1,815 in quarterly licensing fees and $3,750 in annual licensing fees due on July 1, 2015. The unpaid fees, plus penalties and interest, were transferred to the State Controller's Office for collection.

The Gaming Control Board seeks monetary fines and potential disciplinary action against the gaming licenses held by the respondents. The complaint cites violations of multiple Nevada Gaming Commission regulations and statutes, including unsuitable methods of operation and failure to comply with licensing requirements.

The case highlights the Nevada Gaming Commission's strict oversight of gaming operations and enforcement of regulations designed to maintain public confidence in the industry through proper licensing, supervision and fee collection.

Technology Hit - Parlay Betting System Failures

The Nevada Gaming Control Board filed a complaint against CG Technology for systemic failures in its computerized bookmaking system, resulting in thousands of incorrect payouts to betting patrons between 2011 and 2015.

The investigation began when a patron at Silverton Casino Lodge Las Vegas reported being underpaid on a winning round robin parlay wager - his fifth such underpayment. While previous errors were corrected when brought to the casino's attention, the patron decided to alert regulators.

The Board's investigation revealed CG Technology knew its Cantor Sports Book system miscalculated parlay wagers since its 2011 launch. The company only fixed errors when patrons complained, leaving thousands of underpaid winners unaware and uncompensated. The system issues worsened when CSB expanded from mobile to over-the-counter wagers in April 2014.

Between August 2011 and March 2015, the faulty system underpaid winning parlays over 20,000 times totaling approximately $700,000, while overpaying more than 11,000 times for about $100,000. CG Technology could have prevented these errors by disabling the fixed odds option, but chose not to for business reasons.

The Board detailed six counts of violations:

Count One focused on CG Technology's implementation of faulty software leading to incorrect payouts and failure to properly pay underpaid patrons unless they complained.

Count Two addressed the company's failure to notify patrons about the system issues or identify and contact underpaid winners.

Count Three cited CG Technology's inadequate disclosure to regulators about the nature and scope of the software problems.

Count Four detailed the company's lack of cooperation during the investigation, including delayed access to computers and incomplete information sharing.

Count Five involved violations of minimum internal control standards for failing to verify wager authenticity and manually regrade tickets.

Count Six stemmed from accepting six wagers on a mixed martial arts match after its conclusion in January 2016, despite previous warnings about post-event betting.

The complaint marked CG Technology's second major regulatory issue, following a $5.5 million fine in 2014. During settlement of the previous case, the company was warned future violations could result in license revocation.

The Board requested fines and potential action against CG Technology's licenses, registrations, and findings of suitability. It also sought measures to ensure all affected patrons receive accurate payments for their winning wagers.

Silver Peak Restaurant - Ownership Changes

The Nevada Gaming Control Board filed a complaint against Silver Peak Restaurant and Brewery in Reno for multiple violations of gaming regulations related to unauthorized transfers of ownership interests between 2010 and 2014.

The complaint alleges Silver Peak, a restricted gaming licensee since 1999, failed to obtain required Nevada Gaming Commission approval for several ownership transfers despite previous warnings in 2004 and 2007 about compliance requirements.

According to the complaint, the violations began in July 2010 when Robert Garvie's 4% ownership stake was diluted to 3.2% after he opted not to participate in a capital call. The ownership interests of David Silverman and Trent Schmidt increased proportionally as they covered Garvie's portion.

Similar dilutions occurred with Sergio Corado's 4% stake and Gary Silverman's 2% stake, both reduced to 3.2% and 1.6% respectively through the same capital call process.

The complaint details additional unauthorized transfers in 2012, when Corado sold half of his remaining interest to David Silverman for $6,500 and the other half to Schmidt for the same amount. Robert Garvie made similar split sales of his interest to both men for $6,000 each.

In August 2012, John Lundt sold his entire 4% ownership to David Silverman for $24,000 without required approvals. A February 2013 marital separation agreement led to William Thornton receiving a 4% interest, which he transferred to Daniel and Diane Thornton - all without proper authorization.

The Board also cited Silver Peak for submitting incorrect ownership verification forms between 2010 and 2014. The forms, signed under penalty of perjury by Trent Schmidt as General Partner, failed to disclose any of these ownership changes.

Each violation could result in fines up to $100,000 for first offenses and $250,000 for subsequent violations. The Commission may also take action against Silver Peak's gaming license.

The case underscores Nevada gaming regulators' strict oversight of ownership changes in licensed establishments, requiring advance approval to maintain industry integrity and public trust.

D Rock Gaming and Golden Gate Casino - Craps

Nevada gaming regulators filed a complaint against D Rock Gaming (The D), Golden Gate Casino, and Derek Stevens over multiple violations of gaming regulations in 2014-2015.

The most serious incident occurred on January 26, 2015, when Stevens allegedly directed staff at Golden Gate Casino to give $5,000 in gaming chips to a patron without proper documentation or credit procedures. According to the complaint, Stevens told a casino host he wanted "no paper trail" for the transaction.

When approached about the request, a boxman at craps table 01 initially refused to hand over the chips without proper paperwork. The casino shift manager later took over the boxman position and facilitated the exchange, converting $5,000 in $100 black chips to $500 purple chips for the patron.

No credit account had been established for the patron, and no markers were issued or recorded. The transaction resulted in erroneous information being submitted on Golden Gate's Monthly

Gross Revenue Report for February 2015, underreporting gaming revenue by $5,000.

Further complications arose when Golden Gate's records showed a $5,000 payment received on February 7, 2015, for a marker supposedly issued to the same patron on January 25, 2015. However, casino records showed no markers were issued on those dates.

The regulators also found Golden Gate misreported the $5,000 credit issuance on its March 2015 statistical report, claiming it occurred at blackjack table 07 rather than craps table 01.

At The D Casino, separate violations occurred in January 2014 when the Director of Hosts and Chief Operating Officer issued markers of $10,000 and $15,000 respectively to another patron without conducting required credit checks.

The Nevada Gaming Control Board cited multiple regulatory violations, including failure to maintain proper records, unsuitable methods of operation, and non-compliance with credit issuance procedures. The board sought fines and potential disciplinary action against the gaming licenses of all parties involved.

The complaint highlighted how the actions violated Nevada's strict gaming regulations designed to maintain public confidence through "honest and competitive" operations free from "criminal and corruptive elements."

Rampart Casino - Intoxicated Gambling

The Nevada Gaming Control Board filed a complaint against Hotspur Casinos Nevada Inc., operating as Rampart Casino at the Resort at

Summerlin, for multiple violations involving an intoxicated patron who lost nearly $13,000 in a single day.

On January 30, 2015, a patron began gambling at Rampart Casino at 11:38 a.m., starting a series of events leading to four separate regulatory violations. Over the next five and a half hours, casino staff served the patron eleven glasses of red wine - nine from one cocktail server and two from another.

The patron's visible intoxication became evident through several behaviors: spilling drinks, staggering, walking unsteadily, losing balance, struggling with card handling, and inability to stand straight. Despite these clear signs, casino personnel continued allowing the patron to gamble.

Around 5:30 p.m., after another casino patron reported being "slammed into" by the intoxicated individual, casino management finally cut off alcohol service. However, they still permitted the gambling to continue. The patron withdrew more money from an ATM while being monitored by both a security supervisor and surveillance supervisor.

After a dinner break at 7:30 p.m., the patron returned to gamble for another 90 minutes, during which time staff served two more glasses of red wine. By the end of the day, the patron had lost $12,965, with a total cash-in amount of $38,755 and cash-out of $25,790.

The Gaming Control Board cited Rampart Casino with four counts of violations:
- Failure to exercise discretion and sound judgment
- Permitting visibly intoxicated persons to participate in gaming
- Serving complimentary drinks to visibly intoxicated persons
- Failure to comply with gaming regulations and local laws

The Board requested the Nevada Gaming Commission impose monetary fines and take appropriate action against Rampart's gaming licenses. The complaint emphasizes the casino's responsibility to maintain suitable methods of operation and protect public welfare, highlighting how the incident reflects poorly on Nevada's gaming industry.

Perpetual Gaming Suspicious Activity

The Nevada Gaming Control Board filed a complaint against Perpetual Gaming, LLC, revealing multiple violations of gaming regulations and standards. The investigation uncovered a complex web of unlicensed operations and regulatory breaches.

According works of the complaint, Perpetual Gaming allowed unlicensed companies, including Size Matters Gaming (SMG) and Size Matters Gaming, LLC, to manufacture, distribute, and operate slot machines under Perpetual's licenses. The company also permitted an unlicensed manufacturer and distributor to assemble and distribute gaming devices in Nevada.

The investigation discovered Perpetual Gaming participated in foreign gaming operations without proper registration with the Commission. Serial numbers on "Mini-Bertha" slot machines at a manufacturing facility failed to match between cabinet plates and permanent components, violating regulatory requirements.

The Board cited Perpetual Gaming for late reporting of out-of-state gaming device distributions to California casinos. The company missed deadlines for reporting shipments to Cache Creek Casino Resort, Eagle Mountain Casino, and Pechanga Resort and Casino.

In a particularly serious breach, the investigation found no registered gaming employees at Perpetual Gaming, despite its active manufacturing, distribution, and gaming operations in Nevada. While owner John-Martin Meyer claimed workers served in advisory roles without compensation, financial records showed sales commissions and consulting fees were paid.

The complaint outlined thirteen counts of violations, including:
- Allowing unlicensed entities to manufacture gaming devices
- Permitting unauthorized distribution of gaming devices
- Enabling unlicensed entities to operate gaming devices
- Failing to maintain proper serial number documentation
- Missing deadlines for out-of-state distribution reports
- Breaking foreign gaming registration requirements
- Employing unregistered gaming workers
- Neglecting employee reporting requirements
- Maintaining incomplete accounting records
- Missing transaction reports
- Lacking required corporate documentation
- Allowing unauthorized participation in operations

The Board seeks monetary fines for each violation and potential action against Perpetual Gaming's licenses and findings of suitability. The case highlights the complex regulatory framework governing Nevada's gaming industry and the serious consequences of operational violations.

Caesars Palace - Anti-Money Laundering Violations

The Nevada Gaming Control Board filed a complaint against Caesars Entertainment Corporation and its subsidiaries for numerous violations of federal anti-money laundering regulations discovered during an IRS examination.

The investigation, conducted from February to April 2012, revealed approximately 37 areas of noncompliance with the Bank Secrecy

Act at Caesars Palace. After analyzing Caesars' responses to the findings, the IRS deemed the casino's explanations inadequate in 15 of 24 highlighted areas.

According to the complaint, Caesars maintained "highly deficient internal controls" in its private gaming salons, areas catering to the casino's wealthiest and riskiest patrons. These deficiencies allowed secondary patrons to potentially conceal their identities by playing under a primary patron's credit or front money.

The violations extended to Caesars' branch offices abroad, particularly in Asia. The complaint noted zero suspicious activity reports were filed from Asian branches during the examination period, despite these locations routinely accepting payments on markers issued by Caesars.

The Board found Caesars failed to file over 100 suspicious activity reports for various activities, including:
- Team play among unidentified guests in private gaming salons
- Suspicious transactions at branch offices
- Third-party payments from unrelated individuals and businesses
- Structuring of transactions
- Minimal gaming and bill stuffing
- Chip walking
- Observed suspicious patron behavior

In one instance, Caesars acknowledged it should have filed reports for 28 cases where patrons wired funds from business accounts for marker payments and front money deposits exceeding $10,000, but no relationship between the patron and business could be established.

The complaint also cited inadequate Bank Secrecy Act training for employees, resulting in "fundamental misunderstandings" of suspicious transactions. The casino's marketing department obtained information about wealthy patrons but failed to incorporate this data into its anti-money laundering controls.

The Nevada Gaming Commission can impose fines of up to $100,000 for each initial violation and up to $250,000 for subsequent violations. The Commission may also take action against Caesars' gaming licenses.

The case highlights Nevada gaming regulators' ongoing concerns about money laundering in casinos, even after ceding direct oversight of cash transaction reporting to federal authorities in 2007. As Commission Chairman Peter Bernhard stated when discussing these regulations: "The problems addressed are problems important to us not as a state but also as a country."

777 Gaming Hit with 71 Violations

The Nevada Gaming Control Board filed a sweeping complaint against 777 U.S. Inc. and its subsidiaries, alleging 71 violations of gaming regulations across multiple properties in Nevada.

The complaint, filed in September 2015, named Max Casino, Carson Station Hotel/Casino, and Silver State Gaming Inc. as respondents alongside parent company 777 U.S. Inc. The violations spanned from inadequate record-keeping to improper gaming procedures.

At Max Casino, investigators found numerous deficiencies in progressive slot machine monitoring, documentation of jackpots, and currency counting procedures. The casino failed to properly log progressive payoff amounts, maintain explanations for meter reading decreases, and document the distribution of incremental amounts between machines.

The Board discovered Max Casino's slot analysis reports contained incorrect theoretical hold percentages, and large variations between theoretical and actual hold percentages went uninvestigated. In one case, a machine showed an actual hold percentage of 137.35% when theoretical hold should not exceed 25%.

Carson Station faced similar violations, including improper progressive meter logging and incorrect stock certificate documentation. Investigators found slot attendants could potentially produce fraudulent payout forms up to $625 and access cage cashier swipe cards without proper authorization.

Silver State Gaming's violations included failure to reimburse several businesses for slot fees dating back to 2007, improper licensing of corporate officers, and inadequate inventory control of slot machines.

The company's president, Rory Bedore, served as president, treasurer and secretary since 2006 without obtaining proper gaming licenses for these positions.

Multiple properties failed to maintain required bankroll calculations, report capital contributions, and follow proper procedures for player tracking systems and promotional programs.

The complaint highlighted recurring violations previously cited in Board letters from 2012 and 2013, demonstrating ongoing compliance issues across the organization's properties.

The Gaming Control Board sought monetary fines and potential disciplinary action against the gaming licenses held by 777 U.S. Inc. and its subsidiaries. The exact amounts of the proposed fines were not specified in the complaint.

The case underscored the Nevada Gaming Commission's strict requirements for proper gaming operations, accurate record-keeping, and maintaining public confidence in the state's gaming industry.

Holder Group's Gaming Properties – Cash Reserves

State gaming regulators filed a complaint against Harold Douglas Holder and his gaming properties, citing numerous violations across multiple locations including Sharkey's Nugget in Gardnerville and Sundance Casino in Winnemucca.

The Nevada Gaming Control Board uncovered a pattern of bankroll deficiencies at both properties between October and November 2014. At Sharkey's Nugget, inspectors found cash shortfalls ranging from $291 to $17,378. The Sundance Casino also failed to maintain required cash reserves, with deficiencies up to $4,960.

Beyond monetary issues, both establishments lost their player club points systems in September 2014. Initially telling patrons to wait a few days for restoration, the properties later informed customers their accumulated points had been permanently lost.

Record-keeping violations plagued both locations. Sharkey's failed to maintain essential documentation, including:
- Drop/count paperwork from April 2013 through June 2013
- Payout information from April 2014 through November 2014
- Original cage documents spanning April 2013 to November 2014
- Progressive meter logs for fall 2014
- Slot analysis reports comparing actual to theoretical hold percentages

The Board discovered Sharkey's had reduced progressive slot machine payoffs to zero without proper authorization or documentation. The property also failed to keep detailed records of taxable sales during live entertainment periods.

Sundance Casino showed similar compliance issues, failing to produce reports on expired wagering vouchers or properly account for them in revenue reports from September through November 2014. The casino also stopped producing required slot analysis reports after its system crashed in September 2014.

The Nevada Gaming Commission can impose fines up to $100,000 per initial violation and up to $250,000 for subsequent violations. The Commission may also take action against the gaming licenses held by the properties.

This case highlights the Gaming Control Board's ongoing efforts to ensure gaming establishments maintain proper financial reserves and accurate records to protect public interest and maintain the integrity of Nevada's gaming industry.

Las Vegas Sands Corp - Foreign Operations

The Nevada Gaming Control Board filed a complaint against Las Vegas Sands Corp. and its subsidiaries over failures in their Chinese and Macau operations between 2006 and 2011, revealing a pattern of questionable practices and inadequate controls.

The complaint stems from a 2016 Securities and Exchange Commission (SEC) order where Las Vegas Sands paid a $9 million civil penalty for violating the Foreign Corrupt Practices Act's internal controls and books and records provisions.

At the heart of the matter was the company's relationship with a Chinese consultant who claimed to be a former government official. Through this consultant, Las Vegas Sands transferred more than

$62 million in a series of transactions often lacking proper documentation or authorization.

The consultant helped orchestrate several controversial deals, including the purchase of a Chinese basketball team named "Wei Li Xin" - meaning "good fortune" and sounding like "Venetian" in Chinese. The team purchase was structured through the consultant because the Chinese Basketball Association wouldn't allow a gaming company to own a team directly.

Despite internal warnings about accountability issues, Las Vegas Sands continued transferring funds to the consultant. A Senior Director of Finance raised concerns after learning the consultant had allegedly paid a senior CBA official, but was later placed on administrative leave and terminated.

The complaint also details the company's troubled venture into Beijing real estate. Las Vegas Sands spent approximately $43 million to purchase a building dubbed the "Adelson Center," intended as a business center to help U.S. companies entering China. The project lacked basic business analysis and was later shuttered.

In Macau, the company's operations showed similar control deficiencies. The Venetian Macao failed to properly track complimentary services given to government officials and politically exposed persons. The company also selected a ferry service provider partially owned by a state-owned company, citing political advantages.

The Gaming Control Board argues these actions violated Nevada gaming regulations by reflecting poorly on the state's reputation and deterring industry development. The complaint seeks disciplinary action and potential fines against Las Vegas Sands and its subsidiaries.

A second count in the complaint focuses on the company's handling of high-roller Zhenli Ye Gon, who lost over $90 million at the Venetian between 2005 and 2007. Mexican authorities later seized $207 million from Ye Gon's home during a raid. The board alleges Las Vegas Sands failed to properly monitor and report suspicious transactions related to Ye Gon's gambling activities.

The board is asking the Nevada Gaming Commission to take action against the company's licenses and impose monetary penalties for each violation of state gaming laws and regulations.

Foxy Girls Bar - String of Violence

The Nevada Gaming Commission filed an amended complaint against Herda's Bar and Grill Inc., doing business as Foxy Girls, following numerous incidents of violence, criminal activity, and regulatory violations at the Las Vegas establishment.

The bar, which obtained its restricted gaming license in 1986, transformed into an adult entertainment venue in 2001. Problems began escalating in August 2013 when new management started attracting a different clientele.

Between August 2013 and January 2015, Las Vegas Metropolitan Police Department (Metro) responded to multiple serious incidents, including shootings, fights, and gang-related activity. In one incident on January 1, 2014, officers responded to reports of gunshots at the establishment. A similar incident occurred exactly one year later when rival gang members engaged in an armed confrontation outside the venue.

The January 2015 incident revealed security guards were illegally carrying firearms, with one guard discharging rounds into the air before attempting to conceal weapons from police. Officers discovered a stolen handgun, an AR15 rifle, and a shotgun among the security staff's possessions.

The complaint outlines multiple regulatory violations. Count One alleges Foxy Girls and Nicholas Herda received at least 12 notices of non-compliance with Clark County Code and four misdemeanor citations, violating Nevada Gaming Commission Regulation 5.011(8).

Count Two focuses on the establishment's operations attracting individuals with criminal histories, creating an unsafe environment and straining police resources. The complaint alleges these actions violated NRS 463.170 and Gaming Commission Regulations.

Count Three addresses the illegal possession and discharge of firearms by employees, while Count Four centers on staff attempting to hinder Metro's investigation of the January 2015 incident.

The Gaming Control Board seeks monetary fines for each violation and potential action against the respondents' gaming licenses and suitability findings. The case highlights the gaming industry's strict regulatory requirements and the consequences of failing to maintain proper security and operational standards.

Metro officers repeatedly met with Nicholas Herda to discuss policing issues and notify him of Clark County Code requirements, but problems persisted, forcing police to maintain a constant presence near the property.

Searchlight Nugget Casino - Violations in Nevada

The Nevada Gaming Control Board filed a complaint against Verlie May Doing, operating as Searchlight Nugget Casino, alleging seven counts of regulatory violations. The complaint stems from an interim audit conducted on January 15, 2014, revealing ongoing compliance issues despite previous disciplinary actions.

In Count One, the casino failed to comply with a September 2013 license condition requiring it to contract with a licensed slot route operator. The condition mandated the operator perform all drops, fills, counts, and other slot machine operations. As of May 30, 2014, Searchlight Nugget continued performing these functions internally.

During a January 15 coin count observation, inspectors found the count room door left open, violating Internal Control Procedures (ICP) Slots requirements outlined in Count Two.

Count Three cited discrepancies in theoretical hold percentages for multiple slot machines (#408, #411, #423, and #430), where calculated averages did not match slot analysis reports.

The Board discovered in Count Four slot analysis reports from October 2013 through March 2014 showed identical month-to-date and year-to-date figures for coin-in, drop, jackpots, and win information, indicating inaccurate system computations.

Count Five addressed staffing violations at the casino, which operates over 50 slot machines. The Assistant Manager/Slot Auditor performed both accounting procedures and manual slot payout transactions, violating independence requirements.

A $5,155.46 variance between casino accountability and general ledger figures from December 31, 2013, formed the basis of Count Six.

The final count revealed multiple bankroll calculation errors in November and December 2013. The casino incorrectly included coins, tokens, slot payouts, and personal checks in Cash On Hand calculations, while improperly counting tokens and slot payouts in Next Business Day figures.

The Gaming Control Board seeks monetary fines and potential action against the casino's gaming licenses. This complaint follows previous violations cited in 2005, 2007, 2009, 2011, and 2013, demonstrating a pattern of ongoing compliance issues.

Quick Stop Food Mart - Cigarette Sting

A Las Vegas convenience store holding a restricted gaming license found itself in hot water after repeatedly purchasing what employees believed to be stolen cigarettes from an undercover police officer.

The Nevada Gaming Control Board filed a complaint against Quick Stop Food Mart and its owner Bharat Vasant Patel following an investigation sparked by a retailer's tip in November 2012. The retailer informed Las Vegas Metropolitan Police Department merchandise stolen from their store was being sold at Quick Stop.

In response, LVMPD launched an undercover operation, with two grocery stores providing marked cartons of cigarettes. Between January 10-15, 2013, Quick Stop employees and Patel purchased cigarettes from an undercover officer on three separate occasions.

The first purchase occurred on January 10, when store clerk Paramjit Singh and employee Gita Patel bought five cartons for $100 - less than half the wholesale price. The undercover officer hinted at the illicit nature of the goods, mentioning items "walking out the back door."

Four days later, in a more cautious transaction, Gita Patel orchestrated the purchase of 15 cartons for $220 in the parking lot.

She inspected the cigarettes away from the store before completing the deal. The wholesale value exceeded $746.

The final purchase took place January 15, when Bharat Patel and Gita Patel collaborated to buy 17 cartons for $200. The undercover officer explicitly suggested the cigarettes came from multiple store thefts, with Gita Patel agreeing to future purchases.

On January 29, an undercover detective bought one pack of the marked cigarettes from Quick Stop. Two days later, police executed a search warrant, discovering 42 cartons of marked cigarettes still in inventory.

The criminal case concluded in December 2013. Gita Patel pleaded guilty to disorderly conduct and petit larceny, receiving a suspended sentence and $1,000 fine. Paramjit Singh and Bharat Patel each pleaded to disorderly conduct, receiving suspended sentences and fines.

The Gaming Control Board's complaint cited multiple violations, including failure to maintain suitable operations and conduct detrimental to Nevada's gaming industry. The board sought fines and potential action against Quick Stop's gaming license.

Most telling: Quick Stop paid $11-20 per carton for cigarettes worth $45-51 wholesale. The store stood to make profits up to eight times higher than legitimate retailers, while ignoring requirements to purchase only from licensed wholesalers.

Klondike Sunset Casino Bankroll Violations

The Nevada Gaming Control Board filed a complaint against Klondike Sunset Casino in Henderson for repeatedly failing to maintain required minimum bankroll amounts over an 11-month period in 2013.

According to the complaint, the casino's troubles began in February 2013 when a Board verification revealed cash deficiencies of $12,086 in "Cash on Hand" and $25,706 in "Next Business Day" funds. The casino subsequently submitted weekly bankroll reports showing additional deficits of $6,800 and $5,513 in March.

Despite receiving a violation letter from the Board in March 2013, Klondike Sunset continued to struggle with maintaining adequate funds. In July, inspectors found new shortfalls of $8,957 and $10,106. When Board agents returned days later, they discovered deficiencies of $7,772 and $9,125, prompting the owner to add $11,000 to the casino safe during the inspection.

The pattern persisted through August, when a general review uncovered shortages of $8,053 and $12,000. The Board issued an Order to Show Cause in September, but the violations continued. An October verification revealed deficits of $11,586 and $16,233. Though management added $15,000 to cover these amounts, a $1,233 shortage remained.

By December 2013, the casino was still falling short, with a "Next Business Day" deficiency of $2,623.

The complaint outlines eight separate counts against Klondike Sunset, each citing violations of Nevada gaming regulations requiring casinos to maintain sufficient bankroll to protect patrons against defaults in gaming debts. The Board alleges the casino failed to meet licensing standards and operated in a manner "inimical to public health, safety, morals, good order and general welfare."

The Board is seeking monetary fines and potential action against Klondike Sunset's gaming license. Under Nevada law, the casino could face fines up to $100,000 for an initial violation and up to $250,000 for subsequent violations.

Peppermill Casinos - Slot Machine Spying

The Nevada Gaming Control Board filed a complaint against Peppermill Casinos, Inc. for conducting unauthorized surveillance of competitors' slot machines through an employee who accessed sensitive gaming data.

According to the complaint, Ryan Tors, a corporate analyst for Peppermill Casinos, entered the Grand Sierra Resort and Casino in Reno on July 12, 2013. While on the premises, he inserted a slot machine "reset" key into several of the casino's machines. The key allowed access to critical information including theoretical hold percentages, diagnostic data, play history, and game configuration.

Security personnel at Grand Sierra Resort detained Tors and contacted gaming regulators, triggering an investigation. The probe revealed Tors had been systematically gathering theoretical hold percentage information from slot machines at numerous competing casinos since at least 2011.

The affected properties included major Reno-area casinos like the Eldorado Hotel and Casino, Circus Circus Hotel/Casino, and the Atlantis Casino Resort. The scheme also targeted casinos in Sparks, Sun Valley, and Wendover, Nevada.

Most damaging to Peppermill was the investigation's finding its management knew about, approved, and directed Tors to obtain the sensitive slot machine data from competitors.

The complaint outlines three counts against Peppermill Casinos. Count One focuses on the Grand Sierra Resort incident, while Count

Two encompasses the systematic gathering of data from at least ten competitor casinos over multiple years. Count Three specifically addresses management's role in instructing the employee to conduct the unauthorized surveillance.

Each count alleges violations of Nevada gaming regulations requiring licensees to maintain suitable operations and avoid activities "inimical to public health, safety, morals, good order and general welfare." The complaint argues Peppermill's actions reflected poorly on Nevada's gaming industry and failed to meet proper standards of conduct.

The Gaming Control Board seeks monetary fines and potential disciplinary action against Peppermill's gaming licenses. The company operates five Nevada properties: the Peppermill Hotel & Casino in Reno, Western Village in Sparks, Rainbow Club and Casino in Henderson, and both the Rainbow Casino and Peppermill Inn & Casino in West Wendover.

Aria Resort & Casino - High-Roller Privacy Incident

The Nevada Gaming Control Board filed an amended complaint against Aria Resort & Casino following an October 2013 incident where gaming regulators were allegedly blocked from observing a high-stakes roulette game.

Two Gaming Control Board agents attempted to watch gameplay at a roulette table in Aria's high-limit Salon Prive room. Standing 5-7 feet away, they were approached by an Aria floor supervisor who informed them two players did not want to be watched. When an agent asked if all games were open to the public, the supervisor said observation was "not welcome" and threatened to call security to block their view of the table.

The complaint highlights this wasn't Aria's first violation. The Board previously sent violation letters to Aria in March and October 2010 for similar incidents. After each letter, Aria claimed to have taken corrective actions to prevent future occurrences.

The issue extended beyond Aria. In March 2013, the Board issued an Order to Show Cause to MGM Resorts International, which owns 50% of Aria through subsidiaries, regarding public access violations at another MGM property. MGM's response assured regulators all its luxury properties, including Aria, understood "the need for vigilance in ensuring public access to gaming."

The Board alleges Aria's actions violated state law requiring gaming activities remain open to the public. The complaint cites multiple violations of gaming regulations, including:

- Restricting access to gaming contrary to Nevada law
- Conducting operations in a manner harmful to public welfare
- Failing to exercise sound judgment to prevent incidents damaging to Nevada's gaming industry
- Not complying with state laws and regulations
- Operating below proper standards of custom and decency

The Board seeks monetary fines and potential disciplinary action against Aria's gaming licenses. Under Nevada law, the Gaming Commission can levy fines up to $100,000 for initial violations and $250,000 for subsequent violations.

Stagestop Casino - Employee Registration Failures

The Nevada Gaming Commission launched disciplinary action against Best Bet Products, Inc., operating as Stagestop Casino in Pahrump, Nevada, following a compliance review revealing widespread employee registration violations.

During a June 30, 2013 review, state gaming officials discovered seven out of nine bartenders at Stagestop Casino were not properly registered as gaming employees. The violations ranged from two weeks to approximately three and a half years of non-compliance.

Two of these bartenders, while registered gaming employees elsewhere, failed to file required change of location notifications for their work at Stagestop. The investigation also uncovered three former gaming employees who had worked without proper registration.

Further compounding the violations, Stagestop Casino had neglected to submit mandatory hire reports since October 2010. When confronted by a Gaming Control Board agent on July 8, 2013, Stagestop's President Shawn Paul Holmes admitted the casino had not monitored gaming employee registrations for several years.

The Gaming Control Board filed two counts against Stagestop Casino and Holmes. Count One cited violations of state law and gaming regulations regarding employee registration requirements. Count Two addressed the casino's failure to submit required hire reports, marking a significant breach of operational compliance.

The Commission could impose fines up to $100,000 for each initial violation and up to $250,000 for subsequent violations. Additional penalties might include action against Stagestop's gaming licenses.

The case underscores Nevada's strict regulatory framework for gaming employees, designed to maintain public confidence and protect the industry's integrity. State law mandates all gaming employees must be registered, with proper documentation filed within 10 days of employment changes.

Golden Route Operations - Multiple Gaming Violations

The Nevada Gaming Commission filed a complaint against Golden Route Operations LLC (GRO) for operating slot machines without proper licensing and sharing gaming revenue with an unlicensed entity.

The case stems from a September 2011 Participation Agreement between GRO and Million Dollar Entertainment & Advertising, Inc. (MDEA) to place and operate slot machines at The 25 Bar & Grill in Las Vegas. Under the agreement, GRO would give MDEA a percentage of gaming revenue from the machines.

GRO initially placed four slot machines at the location, later increasing to ten machines in December 2011. The company claimed MDEA's President Paul Bowman misrepresented himself as the General Manager of The 25 Bar & Grill with authority to enter agreements on behalf of the owner, BJ Property, LLC (BJP).

However, MDEA had previously entered into a management agreement with BJP, giving MDEA full control of The 25 Bar & Grill operations. When GRO signed the Participation Agreement, Bowman was acting as MDEA's President, not as BJP's representative.

The complaint outlines three main violations:

Count One alleges GRO violated state law by operating slot machines without required licensing. Nevada law mandates a restricted gaming license for operating 15 or fewer slot machines at an establishment. Neither GRO nor MDEA held such a license.

Count Two charges GRO with unlawfully receiving revenue shares from an unlicensed gaming operation. The company collected profits from the slot machines despite lacking proper licensing.

Count Three accuses GRO of allowing an unlicensed person to share in gaming revenue. GRO paid MDEA $20,552.65 in gaming revenue, though MDEA lacked state licensing to receive such payments.

The Gaming Control Board seeks financial penalties and possible action against GRO's gaming licenses. Under Nevada law, fines can reach $100,000 for each initial violation and up to $250,000 for subsequent violations.

The case highlights Nevada's strict gaming regulations and the requirement for proper licensing at all levels of gaming operations. The Commission emphasizes gaming licenses cannot be transferred and all parties receiving gaming revenue must be properly licensed.

Flamingo Investments and Andre Agassi

The Nevada Gaming Control Board filed a complaint against Flamingo Investments LLC, operator of the Sedona Lounge in Las Vegas, along with tennis legend Andre Agassi and other parties for multiple gaming regulation violations involving undisclosed ownership transfers and filing false documents.

According to the complaint, the violations began in 2009 when Adam Corrigan, a trustee who previously faced gaming disciplinary actions in the 1990s, failed to report significant ownership changes in required annual filings. The Board alleges Corrigan submitted forms under penalty of perjury which omitted a major ownership transfer - the Marquis Trust's 31.5% stake in Flamingo Investments moved to the Corrigan Trust.

The complaint outlines three main counts against the respondents:

In Count One, regulators cited violations for failing to disclose ownership changes on mandatory verification forms between 2009-

2011. Beyond the Marquis Trust transfer, the forms also omitted ARI Restaurants LLC's name change to AKA Restaurants LLC until 2012, though the change occurred in 2009.

Count Two focuses on unapproved transfers of gaming interests. The complaint alleges the Rogers Trust transferred its 50% stake in AKA to the Agassi Trust in March 2009 without required Gaming Commission approval. Similarly, the Marquis Trust's transfer to the Corrigan Trust also lacked proper authorization. Both Corrigan and Agassi only submitted applications for these transfers in late 2012 and early 2013.

In Count Three, regulators cited violations for filing false documents with the Nevada Secretary of State. The annual filings from 2003-2012 listed Corrigan personally as Flamingo's manager, though the Gaming Commission had licensed the Corrigan Trust in this role. The 2013 filing continued this discrepancy.

The Board seeks monetary fines for each violation and potential action against the gaming licenses held by the respondents. The case highlights Nevada regulators' strict oversight of gaming ownership changes and documentation requirements, designed to maintain industry integrity and public trust.

For Corrigan, this marks his third encounter with gaming regulators, following previous disciplinary actions in 1992 and 1998 involving improper stock issuance and gaming access violations at other establishments.

Ultra New Town Tavern - Possible License Revocation

The Nevada Gaming Control Board filed a complaint against Ultra New Town Tavern and its operator Tarra Lorraine Green Jackson, citing thirteen counts of regulatory violations spanning from surveillance system deficiencies to failure in maintaining proper financial records.

The Las Vegas establishment, located at 600 West Jackson Avenue, has a history of regulatory issues dating back to 1998, including three unsuitable methods of operation cases and two orders to show cause. In 2009, the Gaming Commission added new conditions to address previous problems, requiring slots-only operation and independent accounting services with monthly reporting requirements.

According to the complaint, investigations revealed Jackson and Ultra New Town failed to report employee terminations for twelve people still registered as gaming employees. The Board discovered this discrepancy during a December 2012 review, and despite notifications in February 2013, the issue remained uncorrected.

The establishment's surveillance system fell short of multiple requirements. Inspections in April 2012 found an unapproved Digital Video Recorder system recording at 25 frames per second instead of the required 30, missing system failure alarms, and no staff proficient in operating the equipment. Despite repeated notifications and visits from Gaming Board agents, these issues persisted into 2013.

Financial oversight proved particularly problematic. The tavern failed to submit required monthly financial statements since December 2010, violating a specific license condition. Employee reports for September 2011, March 2012, and September 2012 were never filed. The company's status with the Secretary of State stood revoked after failing to file its 2012 Annual List of Officers and Directors.

Record-keeping violations included inability to produce casino accountability documents from June 2012 and missing documentation for an $8,804.05 deposit from December 2011. The general ledger remained unprepared since December 2010, affecting various required financial reconciliations.

The complaint also cited violations in basic gaming operations. The establishment's EZ Route system failed to identify cashiers properly, and shift-end reports lacked required signatures. A vault containing $4,680 in tokens and $8,287 in chips went uncounted since December 2010.

In November 2012, investigations revealed bankroll deficiencies of $2,883 for current day operations and $13,512 for next business day requirements, with no calculations prepared between May and September 2012.

The Gaming Control Board seeks monetary penalties for each violation and potential action against the establishment's gaming licenses. The case highlights ongoing regulatory compliance issues at Ultra New Town Tavern despite previous enforcement actions and additional license conditions.

Casino Fandango Owner - Unauthorized Transfer

The Nevada Gaming Control Board filed a complaint against Casino Fandango, LLC and its parent company Carson Gaming, LLC for multiple violations related to licensing requirements and unauthorized transfers of ownership.

According to the complaint, Garry Vincent Goett, who holds a 98.90% interest in Carson Gaming as a licensed Manager and Member, appointed Courtney Edwin Cardinal as a manager of Carson Gaming on February 21, 2012. The appointment violated state regulations when Cardinal failed to apply for required gaming licenses within the mandatory 30-day window. Goett also did not ensure Cardinal filed the necessary applications.

The violations continued when Goett transferred a one percent ownership stake in Carson Gaming to Cardinal without first reporting the terms to the Gaming Control Board or obtaining approval from the Nevada Gaming Commission, as required by law.

In a third violation, Cardinal received cash distributions from Carson Gaming in April, May and July 2012 based on his one percent ownership, despite not being licensed, found suitable, or registered with gaming regulators.

The Gaming Control Board cited these actions as violations of Nevada Gaming Commission regulations and state laws, including NRS 463.5735, NRS 463.5733, and NRS 463.162. The complaint seeks monetary fines for each violation and potential action against the companies' gaming licenses and registrations.

Casino Fandango operates as a nonrestricted gaming establishment at 3800 South Carson Street in Carson City, Nevada. Carson Gaming owns 100% of Casino Fandango and is registered as its holding company with the Gaming Commission.

The state filed the three-count complaint on May 3, 2013, emphasizing these actions constituted "unsuitable methods of operation" under gaming regulations designed to protect public confidence in Nevada's gaming industry.

Cock 'N Bull Casino - Multiple Gaming Violations

The Nevada Gaming Control Board filed a complaint against Ellis Lee Garner, sole proprietor of Cock 'N Bull casino in Fallon, Nevada, alleging multiple violations of gaming regulations and unsuitable business practices.

The investigation, spanning from July 2011 to March 2012, revealed a pattern of non-compliance and uncooperative behavior. The casino failed to submit required surveillance plans, maintain operational gaming machines, and properly document progressive jackpot changes.

Board agents encountered significant resistance when attempting to address these issues. During one interaction, Garner dismissed their concerns by asking, "Don't you have bigger things to worry about?" The casino's manager, Eugena K. Bass, displayed similar reluctance to cooperate, often proving difficult to reach and evasive in communications.

A particularly concerning issue was the prolonged disrepair of slot machines. Agents found approximately 15-20 machines consistently out of service over multiple visits. When questioned, Garner claimed he couldn't find a slot technician in Fallon due to the poor economy. However, a confidential source later discovered the casino had turned away potential technicians, contradicting these claims.

The complaint outlines five specific counts:

Count One alleges the casino failed to surrender its gaming license after closing all games for more than a month, violating NGC Regulation 9.010(2).

Count Two focuses on unsuitable methods of operation, citing the casino's failure to cooperate with gaming authorities and maintain proper standards.

Count Three addresses the casino's two-decade failure to submit required surveillance plans and diagrams, which was only remedied after three months of repeated contact attempts by the Board.

Count Four targets the casino's violation of maintaining slot machines in suitable condition, with numerous machines remaining inoperative for extended periods.

Count Five involves the failure to document and explain a decrease in progressive jackpot meters, violating record-keeping requirements.

The Gaming Control Board seeks multiple penalties, including potential license revocation and monetary fines up to $100,000 for initial violations and $250,000 for subsequent violations.

Throughout the investigation, agents documented a consistent pattern of delayed responses, inadequate solutions, and what they described as "a general disregard and lack of concern" toward gaming regulations and Board authority.

Searchlight Nugget Casino – Bankroll Computign

The Nevada Gaming Commission filed a 27-count complaint against Verlie May Doing, operating as Searchlight Nugget Casino, for numerous violations of gaming regulations between April 2010 and June 2012.

The complaint reveals a history of previous violations, with similar issues cited in complaints from 2009 and 2011, as well as violation letters from 2007 and 2005. Despite these warnings, the casino failed to maintain compliance with state gaming laws and procedures.

Among the most serious violations, investigators found the casino left filled drop carts unattended in a dumbwaiter during coin collection. The count room remained unlocked during currency counts, and currency drop documentation was improperly stored with unverified proceeds.

The casino failed to maintain accurate records for 14 new slot machines and made unauthorized changes to five others. Theoretical hold worksheets were missing for 12 machines and inaccurate for six others. The facility also failed to verify manufacturer specifications when installing 17 new slot machines.

Statistical reports showed significant errors, including overstated coin-in amounts due to broken meters and input mistakes. In one instance, the coin-in amount was overstated by $158,244.33 for a single machine. The casino was aware of errors in their Simco slot system but took no corrective action.

Key security posed another concern, with lost slot machine and currency drop box keys going uninvestigated. The casino failed to perform required sensitive key inventories for slots, table games, and card games in 2011.

The complaint also cited violations of a previous variance allowing only the owner and general manager to count the cage vault alone. Investigators found the assistant controller performed solo counts 15 out of 25 days in June 2012.

Other violations included failure to compute monthly bankroll requirements as mandated and not reporting an $84,700.38 increase in the capital drawing account, which potentially represented an unreported contribution.

The Gaming Commission seeks monetary fines for each violation and potential action against the casino's gaming licenses. The case highlights ongoing compliance issues despite multiple previous enforcement actions and warnings from regulators.

Bally Gaming Hit with 28 Violations

The Nevada Gaming Control Board filed a complaint against Bally Gaming, Inc., doing business as Bally Technologies, alleging multiple violations of gaming employee registration requirements spanning from late 2012 through mid-2013.

The company, based in Las Vegas, had previously received two violation letters in 2007 and faced an Order to Show Cause later the same year regarding similar registration issues. In 2008, Bally settled a complaint for $65,500 over deficiencies in employee hire reports and registration documentation for 56 gaming employees.

The current complaint outlines 28 separate counts of violations. The first violation stems from Bally's failure to submit required hire reports from October through December 2012.

In a notable case, Rosa Hinojosa, a Human Resources Representative with access to the Board's gaming employee system, continued working after her registration expired on January 23, 2013, until February 5, 2013. The Board had to deactivate her system access due to the expired registration.

The complaint details multiple instances of engineers and software professionals working without proper registration. Lorna Lindstedt worked as an engineer for nearly ten years - from February 2003 to February 2013 - without registration. Other employees worked for months with expired registrations, including Barry Iremonger, whose registration lapsed for over nine months.

Recent hires also lacked proper documentation. The company employed multiple software engineers, including Julie Tuquiero and Mikhak Misaghian, without submitting timely registration applications in mid-2013.

The violations extend to change of employment notices, with Bally failing to submit timely notices for several employees, including Aaron Jones and Mark Mendoza.

The Gaming Control Board seeks monetary fines for each violation and potential action against Bally's gaming licenses. The complaint emphasizes the company's responsibility to maintain proper registration for all gaming employees and its failure to implement adequate compliance measures despite previous violations.

The case highlights ongoing compliance issues in the gaming industry and the Board's efforts to enforce strict employee registration requirements designed to maintain public trust in Nevada's gaming operations.

Jitterbug LLC's Bikini Bar Faces Gaming Violations

A complaint filed by the Nevada Gaming Control Board alleges Jitterbug LLC, operating as The Bikini Bar, and its sole member Lonny Joseph Campos violated state gaming regulations through an unauthorized sale arrangement and improper business operations.

According to the complaint, Bikini Bar entered into a $150,000 agreement with 600 Club LLC on June 26, 2012, to sell substantially all of its assets. The buyers, Paul Wilkes and Joseph Adashek, made two $50,000 payments to Bikini Bar and/or Campos around June 22-26, 2012. These payments violated Nevada Gaming Commission regulations by not being placed in escrow as required.

The agreement allowed 600 Club LLC to operate the business before receiving Nevada Gaming Commission approval. The buyers began running Bikini Bar on July 3, 2012, while the establishment's slot machines remained active through March 27, 2013. During this period, Campos continued receiving slot machine revenue despite no longer operating the primary business - a direct violation of Nevada gaming law.

The Gaming Control Board seeks monetary fines for each violation and potential action against the respondents' gaming licenses. The complaint emphasizes how these actions undermined Nevada's strict gaming regulations designed to maintain public confidence and protect the industry's integrity.

Located at 3355 Spring Mountain Road in Las Vegas, Bikini Bar holds a restricted gaming license, permitting it to operate 15 or fewer slot machines incidental to its primary business. The case highlights Nevada's rigorous oversight of gaming operations and the serious consequences for circumventing regulatory requirements.

The Board filed this disciplinary action through the Nevada Attorney General's office, citing violations of NRS 463.161 and Nevada Gaming Commission Regulation 8.050.

Mandalay Bay - Drug Sales and Prostitution

The Nevada Gaming Commission filed a five-count complaint against Mandalay Bay Resort & Casino in March 2014, following an undercover investigation revealing extensive drug trafficking and prostitution at its Foundation Room ultra lounge.

The investigation, conducted jointly by the State Gaming Control Board and Las Vegas Metropolitan Police Department, uncovered multiple instances of cocaine sales, MDMA distribution, and prostitution solicitation between June and August 2012.

On June 8, 2012, an undercover officer purchased 2.8 grams of cocaine from a House of Blues Foundation Room host at a secluded location in Mandalay Bay. The host informed the officer he regularly sold narcotics to venue patrons and advised cocaine could be used inside the Foundation Room "if careful."

During a July visit, the same host sold an officer 2.7 grams of cocaine and 1.8 grams of MDMA. Two additional hosts and a bottle runner offered to provide drugs on future visits. The investigation revealed staff members actively facilitated drug deals and prostitution services.

In late July, a Foundation Room host arranged for an undercover officer to meet with a non-employee who supplied cocaine and brought two prostitutes. Security officers offered to provide marijuana and prescription pills, while also accommodating requests for private rooms where sexual activity could occur.

The complaint details how a bar back served as a drug source for staff members, selling five MDMA pills to an undercover officer in August. Multiple employees, including hosts, servers, and security personnel, were implicated in arranging drug sales and prostitution services over the two-month period.

The Gaming Commission emphasized Mandalay Bay's responsibility to prevent illegal activities on its premises, regardless of third-party venue operations. The casino had received multiple industry notices between 2006-2012 warning about inappropriate conduct in nightclubs and ultra lounges.

The five-count complaint cited violations of gaming regulations requiring suitable operation methods and prevention of activities bringing discredit to Nevada. The Commission sought monetary fines and potential disciplinary action against Mandalay Bay's gaming license.

At least 10 Foundation Room employees and five non-employees were found to have participated in providing drugs, prostitutes, or facilitating illegal activities during the investigation. Many transactions occurred in public areas of Mandalay Bay, highlighting what regulators called a failure to exercise proper oversight of the venue.

Lucky Club Casino - Employee Registration Rules

The Nevada Gaming Control Board filed a complaint against Lucky Club Casino and Hotel in North Las Vegas for continuing to employ a gaming worker after the Board objected to her registration.

According to documents filed with the Nevada Gaming Commission, the Board objected to the gaming employee registration of Kristen Heiselmann on August 3, 2011. Both Heiselmann and Lucky Club received notification of this objection on the same day.

Over a year later, on September 17, 2012, Board investigators discovered Heiselmann remained employed at Lucky Club in a position requiring gaming registration. The casino had failed to terminate her employment or reassign her to a non-gaming position as required by law.

During the subsequent investigation, a Lucky Club employee made misleading and false statements to Board enforcement agents. The employee claimed certain documents showing the casino's compliance efforts came from a Board employee. However, investigators found no Board employee had provided such documents, and the records did not exist in the Board's system.

The complaint outlines two counts against Lucky Club. Count One alleges violations of state gaming laws and regulations requiring proper employee registration. The casino's continued employment of Heiselmann after the Board's objection violated Nevada Revised Statute 463.335 and Gaming Commission regulations.

Count Two focuses on the false statements made to investigators. The complaint alleges Lucky Club, through its employees' actions, failed to maintain the standards required for gaming licensees and violated regulations requiring truthful communication with gaming agents.

The Gaming Control Board seeks monetary fines for each violation and potential action against Lucky Club's gaming licenses. The case highlights Nevada's strict oversight of gaming employee registration and the serious consequences for casinos failing to comply with regulatory requirements.

Mardi Gras Inn Multiple Gaming Registration

The Nevada Gaming Control Board filed a complaint against J.P.P.J. of Nevada, Inc., operating as Mardi Gras Inn, and its vice president Philippe Francois Jaramillo for multiple violations of gaming employee registration requirements.

The Board had previously warned Mardi Gras Inn about compliance issues, sending an order to show cause in 2005 and violation letters in June 2006, October 2006, and September 2010. Despite the Board offering quarterly classes on proper gaming employee registration since 2006, no Mardi Gras employee attended the training.

The current case began when the Board served an order to show cause on July 5, 2012. In his response, Jaramillo claimed a Board agent told him the company no longer needed to submit monthly written lists of gaming employee changes. However, the Board's investigation revealed this statement was false.

The complaint outlines six specific counts of violations. In Count One, Jaramillo's misrepresentation about receiving permission to stop filing reports constituted an unsuitable method of operation.

Counts Two through Five detail multiple instances of Mardi Gras Inn employing unregistered gaming workers. The company hired Lena Covel, Blair Manchester, and Andrea Ybarra in January 2012 but didn't submit their registration applications until April. Similarly, Jenifer Serrano worked with an expired registration from January to April 2012, and Timothy Craft worked unregistered from January to April 2012. Mark Mesolella worked as a bartender for at least a month with an expired registration.

Count Six addresses Mardi Gras Inn's failure to submit required hire reports from March 2010 through April 2012.

The Board seeks monetary fines for each violation and potential action against the company's gaming licenses. The case highlights the importance of maintaining proper gaming employee registration in Nevada's strictly regulated casino industry.

Palms Casino - Drug Sales and Prostitution

The Nevada Gaming Control Board filed a complaint against FP Holdings L.P., operating as Palms Casino Resort, detailing widespread drug sales and prostitution activities at several nightclubs on the property between March and May 2012.

The investigation, conducted jointly by the Gaming Control Board and Las Vegas Metropolitan Police Department, uncovered multiple instances of cocaine sales, prostitution solicitation, and staff facilitating drug use at Moon Nightclub, Rain Nightclub, Ghostbar Nightclub, and the Ditch Fridays pool party.

On March 16, a host manager at Moon offered to provide prostitutes to an undercover officer, stating price was no object. The same manager later sold the officer 1.9 grams of cocaine. Two weeks later, on March 31, a bottle runner at Rain sold cocaine to the officer twice in one night - first 0.9 grams, followed by 5.1 grams. The employee bragged about selling to other patrons and offered to procure a pound of cocaine for $18,000.

The investigation revealed a pattern of employees enabling illegal activities. Security officers accepted bribes to provide private areas for drug use, with one officer charging $220 to guard a room while an undercover officer pretended to use cocaine. Another security officer drew cabana shades and stood watch to conceal supposed drug use at the pool party.

In total, at least 13 employees of the venues were implicated in providing or offering drugs, arranging prostitution services, or facilitating drug use. The venues - Moon, Rain, Ghostbar and Ditch Fridays - were owned and operated by N-M Ventures LLC and N-M Ventures II LLC, subsidiaries in which Palms held at least 50% ownership during the investigation period.

The Gaming Control Board cited Palms' failure to maintain sufficient control over its premises and prevent activities reflecting poorly on Nevada gaming. The complaint noted the Board had previously warned licensees about nightclub activities through letters sent in 2006, 2009 and 2012, as well as industry training classes which Palms representatives attended.

The 17-count complaint seeks monetary fines and potential action against Palms' gaming license. Each violation falls under Nevada

Gaming Commission Regulation 5.011, which prohibits activities deemed "inimical to public health, safety, morals, good order and general welfare" or those reflecting discredit on the state and gaming industry.

Notable incidents included:
- Multiple cocaine sales ranging from 0.9 to 6.2 grams
- Sale of ecstasy pills and Percocet
- Security staff accepting bribes to facilitate drug use
- Employees actively arranging prostitution services
- Management-level involvement in drug sales

The complaint emphasizes the gaming industry's reliance on public confidence and strict regulation to maintain its integrity. All incidents occurred on Palms property between March 16 and May 11, 2012.

Cantor Gaming Hit - Illegal Betting Operations

The Nevada Gaming Control Board filed an 18-count complaint against Cantor Gaming and its affiliated entities for multiple violations, including enabling illegal messenger betting and failing to prevent key employees from engaging in unlawful gambling activities.

The case centers around Michael Lloyd Colbert, who served as Cantor Gaming's Vice President of Race and Sports Risk Management from July 2011. In October 2012, Colbert was indicted by a New York State Grand Jury on charges of enterprise corruption, money laundering, and conspiracy. He later pleaded guilty to federal conspiracy charges related to illegal gambling operations.

According to the complaint, Colbert used his position at Cantor Gaming to facilitate illegal betting activities. The company allegedly failed to prevent him from participating in an unlawful sports gambling enterprise while supervising a team of employees.

The complaint details how Cantor Gaming accepted approximately $34.3 million in illegal messenger bets from three individuals working on behalf of professional gambler Gadoon Kyrollos, known as "Spanky." Paul Sexton placed about $22 million in wagers, Robert Drexler bet approximately $7.9 million, and Thomas Ludford wagered around $4.4 million - all acting as messenger bettors for Kyrollos.

Additional violations included failing to maintain proper wagering account records, allowing expired gaming employee registrations, and not submitting required hiring reports. The company also permitted race and sports book supervisors to place personal wagers, violating Nevada gaming regulations.

The Board found Cantor Gaming failed to file dozens of mandatory book wagering reports between 2011-2013. In one instance, they allowed off-track pari-mutuel wagers through an agent when the principal was not present, breaking state law.

The complaint seeks monetary fines for each violation and potential action against Cantor Gaming's licenses. The case highlights significant compliance failures in preventing illegal gambling activities and maintaining proper oversight of gaming operations.

Lee Amaitis, who served as President and CEO of multiple Cantor Gaming entities during this period, allegedly knew or should have known about Colbert's illegal activities, according to the complaint.

The extensive violations exposed systemic failures in Cantor Gaming's operations, from employee supervision to record-keeping, leading the Gaming Control Board to pursue disciplinary action to protect Nevada's gaming industry reputation and regulatory framework.

BJ Property and Owner - Las Vegas Bar Case

The Nevada Gaming Control Board filed a complaint against BJ Property LLC, operating as The 25 Bar & Grill, and its owner Burdett Edward Jones for multiple violations of gaming regulations between 2010 and 2012.

The case centers on a questionable management agreement signed in July 2011 between BJ Property and Million Dollar Entertainment & Advertising, Inc. (MDEA). Under the $1.1 million deal, MDEA took complete control of The 25 Bar & Grill's operations, including gambling activities, despite lacking required gaming licenses.

The agreement labeled MDEA as "Buyer/Borrower" and BJ Property as "Seller/Lender," suggesting it was effectively a purchase agreement rather than a management contract. Gaming ceased entirely at the location for approximately two months after MDEA took control.

In September 2011, MDEA partnered with Golden Route Operations, LLC (GRO) to operate slot machines at the establishment. Neither company obtained proper gaming licenses before launching operations. MDEA received percentage-based payments from gaming revenues until December 2011, when Jones regained control due to MDEA's contract breach.

The Gaming Control Board outlined four major violations:

Count I accuses BJ Property and Jones of unlawfully transferring interest in their gaming operation to an unlicensed entity, violating NGC Regulation 8.010(1).

Count II charges them with allowing illegal profit-sharing from gaming operations, breaching NGC Regulation 8.010(2).

Count III alleges they failed to report MDEA's profit-sharing arrangement to regulators quarterly as required by NGC Regulation 5.050.

Count IV cites BJ Property's failure to surrender its gaming license when all games were closed for over a month, violating NGC Regulation 9.010(2).

The Board seeks monetary fines for each violation and potential action against BJ Property's gaming license. The case highlights Nevada's strict oversight of gaming operations and emphasis on proper licensing for all parties involved in gambling revenues.

Caesars Entertainment Properties - Gaming Violations

The Nevada Gaming Control Board filed a complaint against several Caesars Entertainment properties, including Harrah's Las Vegas and Caesars Palace, following a series of underage gambling and drinking incidents between 2011-2012.

In the first incident at Harrah's Las Vegas in August 2011, a 17-year-old gambled at craps tables for over five hours while being served at least six alcoholic beverages. Four separate employees served the minor drinks without checking identification. The minor's gambling spree only ended when Las Vegas Metropolitan Police arrested him on an outstanding warrant.

Another violation occurred at Caesars Palace in November 2011, where a 19-year-old female spent several hours at the property and was served multiple alcoholic beverages without being asked for identification.

The violations continued into January 2012 when a 20-year-old female gambled and drank at Harrah's Las Vegas Piano Bar for approximately two and a half hours. She later played craps for an additional two hours. During her time at the property, she encountered around 20 employees - including bartenders, cocktail servers, floor persons, and dealers - none of whom requested identification.

In May 2012, a 19-year-old male managed to play blackjack at Caesars Palace after a dealer misread his passport, which showed his actual age.

The Gaming Control Board noted these incidents followed previous violation letters sent to Caesars Entertainment regarding similar underage gambling occurrences at their properties. Earlier incidents included an 18-year-old gambling at Caesars Palace in January 2010, a 20-year-old gambling at Rio for nine hours in June 2010, and an 18-year-old gambling at Flamingo in August 2011.

The complaint alleges Caesars Entertainment failed to take sufficient action to prevent these incidents, despite multiple warnings. The Board argues these repeated violations reflect poorly on Nevada's gaming industry and warrant disciplinary action.

The Gaming Control Board is seeking monetary fines and potential action against the properties' gaming licenses. The exact amounts will be determined by the Nevada Gaming Commission within the parameters defined by state law.

Leroy's Horse and Sports - Illegal Race Bets

In March 2012, Leroy's Horse and Sports Place discovered a significant software flaw in their sports betting kiosks during the NCAA basketball tournament. The deficiency allowed patrons to double their deposits by repeatedly pressing the "deposit" button after inserting cash.

Upon finding shortages in cash journals at PT's Place on East Sahara, Leroy's and its affiliate Computerized Bookmaking Systems (CBS) launched an investigation. The review revealed over 30 affected kiosks throughout Las Vegas.

On March 21, the companies identified and fixed the software issue. However, Leroy's upgraded six PT Pub location kiosks before notifying the Nevada Gaming Control Board on March 22. The remaining PT Pub kiosks were modified on March 26, while other locations received upgrades after obtaining verbal approval from the Board's technology division on March 29.

In a separate incident on May 5, 2012, Leroy's accepted Kentucky Derby horse race wagers at four unauthorized locations: Colorado Belle Hotel & Casino, Hooters Casino Hotel, The Poker Palace, and Stockmen's Casino. None of these venues held licenses to accept race wagers.

The Board noted this wasn't Leroy's first offense regarding unauthorized race betting. In 2004, the company received an Order to Show Cause for accepting five Kentucky Derby wagers at an unlicensed location in 2003.

The Gaming Control Board filed two counts against Leroy's. The first count cited violations of regulations 14.290, 14.300, and 5.011(8) for modifying kiosks without prior Board approval. The second count addressed violations of NRS 463.160 and regulation 22.020(1) for accepting race wagers at unlicensed locations.

The Board sought monetary fines and potential action against Leroy's gaming licenses. Under Nevada law, fines could reach $100,000 per initial violation and up to $250,000 for subsequent violations.

Jailhouse Casino Hit with 21 Violations

The Nevada Gaming Control Board filed a complaint against the Estate of Norman Lloyd Goeringer, operating as Jailhouse Motel and Casino in Ely, Nevada, alleging 21 separate violations of gaming regulations and internal control procedures.

The Board's investigation, conducted during March and April 2011, revealed extensive compliance failures. The casino failed to report entities sharing in slot revenue, including P & M Coin and Aristocrat Technologies Inc., for six quarters between 2008 and 2010.

Progressive gaming logs showed missing base amounts and meter readings, while accounting records contained unexplained additions to gross gaming revenue. The casino couldn't produce required documentation, including slot analysis reports and bill-in meter reconciliations for 2009.

Security breaches emerged during the investigation. The drop team left currency acceptor boxes unattended, and slot system passwords allowed single individuals to generate and approve jackpot payouts. Key logs contained initials instead of required signatures.

Technical violations plagued the operation. The casino incorrectly calculated theoretical hold percentages on multiple machines, failed to investigate large variations between theoretical and actual hold percentages, and didn't resolve bill-in meter variances exceeding $7,800 in one instance.

Player tracking and computerized systems went unchecked. The casino neglected quarterly reviews of player point redemptions and employee access listings. Exception reports remained unexamined from May 2007 through February 2011.

The Board emphasized the casino's history of non-compliance, citing a previous complaint from 2008 and an Order to Show Cause from 2006. Despite responding to earlier violations, the casino repeatedly failed to maintain compliance with gaming regulations.

The complaint seeks monetary penalties for each violation and potential action against the casino's gaming license. The Board noted these failures reflect poorly on Nevada's gaming industry and constitute unsuitable methods of operation under state regulations.

This case highlights the Gaming Control Board's ongoing efforts to maintain strict oversight of Nevada's gaming operations through regular audits and enforcement actions.

Ten 99 Club - Abandoned Jackpots

The Nevada Gaming Control Board filed a complaint against La Choy Enterprises, LLC, operating as Ten 99 Club, and its owners Barbara Lynn Hossick and Floyd Paul Hossick III for allegedly abandoning progressive slot machine jackpots after ceasing operations.

According to the complaint filed on January 19, 2012, Ten 99 Club, formerly located at 1099 South Virginia Street in Reno, shut down its gaming operations on June 30, 2011. The establishment held a restricted gaming license at the time.

The Gaming Control Board's Tax and License Division placed a hold on Ten 99 Club's license to prevent any attempted surrender. The core issue centers on $5,471.56 in progressive jackpot funds left unresolved when the business closed.

Under Nevada gaming regulations, casino operators must properly dispose of or make suitable arrangements for progressive jackpot amounts before closing. The Board alleges Ten 99 Club failed to meet these obligations.

The complaint cites violations of Nevada Gaming Commission Regulation 5.011, sections 1, 8, and 10, as well as Regulation 5.110. These regulations require gaming establishments to operate in ways protecting public confidence and comply with all state laws and regulations.

The Board seeks unspecified fines within statutory limits for each violation and potential action against Ten 99 Club's gaming license. Barbara Lynn Hossick and Floyd Paul Hossick III each held 50% ownership stakes in the business.

The case highlights Nevada regulators' strict oversight of progressive jackpot obligations, even for smaller restricted gaming locations. Progressive jackpots represent patron obligations licensees must honor, regardless of operational status.

AA Gaming Employee Registration Failures

The Nevada Gaming Commission filed a complaint against AA Gaming Inc., operating as High Sierra Brewing Co., and Alan H. Adams for numerous regulatory violations spanning from 2008 to 2011.

The Carson City-based nonrestricted licensee, initially licensed in June 2008 under the name Doppelganger's, encountered trouble after failing to meet key employee requirements and gaming registration regulations. The company operated 17 slot machines under specific licensing conditions.

The violations began surfacing in November 2008 when the Gaming Control Board notified AA Gaming of its failure to register gaming employees properly. A similar violation occurred in October 2009. By August 2010, the Board cited the company for additional failures in submitting hire and termination reports, maintaining employee pictures, and filing required forms.

After a brief closure from October 2010 to March 2011, AA Gaming reopened as High Sierra Brewing Co. in February 2011. Despite receiving explicit instructions from Board agents about compliance requirements, the company continued violating regulations.

The complaint outlined five specific counts:

Count One accused AA Gaming of operating without a registered general manager from October 2010 until July 2011, violating a key licensing condition.

Count Two addressed the company's employment of unregistered gaming employees after its February 2011 reopening, with management aware of the violation.

Count Three focused on AA Gaming's failure to notify the Board when employees with access to the Board's online verification system left their positions.

Count Four detailed the company's consistent failure to submit required monthly hiring reports and quarterly termination reports since its initial licensing in 2008.

Count Five cited AA Gaming's failure to submit a mandatory employee report due within 30 days after March 31, 2011.

The Gaming Control Board sought monetary fines for each violation and potential action against the company's gaming licenses. The case highlighted persistent regulatory compliance issues despite multiple warnings from gaming authorities.

Carson Cactus Jack's Casino - Poker Chips

The Nevada Gaming Commission filed a complaint against Carson Cactus Jack's Corporation, operating as Cactus Jack's Senator Club, for repeatedly using unauthorized poker chips in tournaments throughout 2010.

The complaint outlines three separate incidents where the Carson City casino conducted poker tournaments with unapproved chips, violating Nevada Gaming Commission Regulation 12.090. The violations occurred in February, May, and August 2010.

David Scott Tate, through his gaming trust, held full ownership of Cactus Jack's alongside interests in nine other nonrestricted gaming licensees, two periodic gaming locations, a slot route operation, and eight restricted gaming establishments.

The complaint highlights a significant oversight issue. As the sole licensed individual for Cactus Jack's and numerous other gaming locations, Tate failed to maintain adequate control over the casino's operations. The repeated use of unauthorized tournament chips across three separate events demonstrated a pattern of regulatory non-compliance.

Gaming regulations require all chips used in casino establishments to receive written approval from the Gaming Control Board chairman before use. The August 2010 violation included physical evidence, with unauthorized chips submitted as exhibits to the complaint.

The Board emphasized how these violations reflect poorly on Nevada's gaming industry and could harm its development. The repeated nature of the infractions forced regulatory authorities to pursue disciplinary action to protect gaming operations and state inhabitants' welfare.

The complaint seeks monetary penalties for each violation and potential action against the respondents' gaming licenses under NRS 463.310(4). The case underscores Nevada's strict regulatory framework and its emphasis on maintaining public trust in gaming operations through proper oversight and compliance.

Searchlight Nugget Casino Gaming Violations

The Nevada Gaming Commission filed a 25-count complaint against Verlie May Doing, operating as Searchlight Nugget Casino in Searchlight, Nevada, alleging numerous violations of gaming regulations and internal control procedures.

The complaint, stemming from an investigation period between April 2007 and March 2010, revealed a pattern of non-compliance despite previous violations and warnings. The casino had been cited in a 2009 complaint and received violation letters in 2007 and 2005 for similar issues.

Key violations included failure to file employee reports on time, with some reports delayed by months or never submitted. The casino showed significant discrepancies in financial records, including a $2.3 million variance in coin-in reporting and unexplained differences in vault documentation.

Security concerns emerged around key access protocols. The cage cashier had unrestricted access to sensitive keys, while the owner maintained improper access to duplicate keys. The investigation found slot machine auditing procedures were compromised, with one person performing both count recorder and audit functions.

The complaint detailed failures in basic accounting practices. The casino neglected to review slot analysis reports, failed to properly document gaming machine removals, and showed errors in recording coin-in meters affecting 28 of 98 machines.

Table games operations exhibited similar problems. Management didn't review statistical reports, investigate unusual fluctuations, or maintain proper documentation for fill and credit slips. The casino performed unauthorized emergency drops and counts on multiple occasions without reporting them to the Board.

The State Gaming Control Board seeks monetary fines for each violation and possible action against the casino's license. The case highlights ongoing compliance issues despite previous enforcement actions and demonstrates the strict regulatory environment governing Nevada's gaming industry.

The casino's bankroll calculations from August 2009 through March 2010 contained numerous inaccuracies, raising concerns about its financial stability and regulatory compliance. These violations represent breaches of Nevada Gaming Commission regulations designed to maintain public trust and prevent corruption in gaming operations.

This latest complaint follows a $3,000 fine and three license conditions imposed on the casino in 2009 for similar violations, indicating persistent operational and compliance issues at the Searchlight property.

Hard Rock Hotel & Casino - Drug Activity

The Nevada Gaming Control Board filed a complaint against the Hard Rock Hotel & Casino in Las Vegas, revealing widespread drug activity and misconduct by employees at its nightclubs between 2009-2010.

The investigation began after the Board sent warning letters to gaming licensees in 2006 and 2009 about nightclub activities, including drug distribution, violence, and other illegal behavior. Despite attending industry training seminars, the Hard Rock failed to prevent numerous violations discovered during undercover operations.

In November 2009, agents discovered a security officer offering private restrooms for drug use and prostitution at the Body English nightclub. A VIP host also attempted to arrange drug purchases and admitted to being under the influence of ecstasy while working.

Further operations in late 2009 found the same security officer accepting $80 to provide a locked restroom for marijuana use, even requesting a "hit" from undercover agents.

The illegal activity continued after Body English closed and Vanity nightclub opened. In January 2010, a security officer sold ecstasy pills to agents while a VIP host provided additional drugs. The security officer later sold cocaine to detectives.

By summer 2010, the investigation revealed deeper involvement of supervisory staff. A security supervisor was identified as a source of drugs for other employees to sell to patrons. Multiple VIP hosts and security officers were implicated in cocaine and ecstasy sales, with some transactions occurring in casino parking garages.

Several employees agreed to cooperate with investigators after being confronted with charges. They detailed how private restrooms were regularly provided for drug use and sex, with supervisors facilitating drug deals through subordinate staff.

The complaint cited eight separate violations of Nevada Gaming Commission regulations, focusing on unsuitable methods of operation and failure to maintain proper standards. The Board alleged Hard Rock knew or should have known about the illegal activities but failed to prevent them.

The Commission considered fines and potential action against Hard Rock's gaming licenses. The complaint highlighted how the criminal behavior persisted even after the casino received warnings and training about nightclub enforcement.

Capado Gaming Corp - Slot Machine Records

In a complaint filed September 30, 2010, the Nevada Gaming Control Board brought disciplinary action against Capado Gaming Corporation for failing to maintain required records of slot machine sales.

The Las Vegas-based gaming distributor, headquartered at 1541 West Oakey Boulevard, came under scrutiny after an investigation revealed incomplete documentation of a 2008 transaction. According to sales records obtained by the Board, Capado sold five slot machines to Camptown, LTD., operating as Crosby's, a restricted gaming establishment in Incline Village, Nevada.

When Board investigators requested serial number records for these machines, Capado was unable to produce them as required by Nevada Gaming Commission Regulation 14.170(3). The company had to contact Crosby's to examine the physical machines to determine their serial numbers.

The Board's complaint emphasizes the gaming industry's vital importance to Nevada's economy and highlights strict regulations requiring detailed record-keeping by licensed distributors. Under state law, gaming device distributors must maintain written documentation of all distributions, including serial numbers, approval numbers, and customer information.

The complaint seeks monetary penalties for each violation and potential disciplinary action against Capado's distributor's license. Nevada Gaming Commission will determine the final sanctions based on the parameters defined in NRS 463.310(4).

The case underscores Nevada's commitment to maintaining strict oversight of gaming device distribution through comprehensive documentation requirements, ensuring accountability in the state's gaming industry.

Caesars Palace - High-Roller's Dancing Incident

The Nevada Gaming Control Board filed a complaint against Desert Palace, Inc., operating as Caesars Palace, following a peculiar incident in their high-limit baccarat room on October 10, 2009.

According to the complaint, a patron at Caesars Palace engaged in unusual behavior over a 45-minute period while gambling in what was supposed to be a private gaming salon but was being used for public gaming. The guest climbed onto the baccarat table multiple times, walked across it, and even danced on its surface while placing wagers.

The complaint details three separate instances where the patron mounted the table. During the first occurrence, the player climbed from his chair onto the table, walked across it to place baccarat wagers, before returning to stand on his chair. In a second incident, the patron again scaled the table, this time adding dancing to his repertoire while continuing to place bets. The third time, the guest walked across the table before descending onto a chair.

Most concerning to regulators was the casino staff's response - or lack thereof. The complaint states Caesars personnel failed to intervene or stop the patron's behavior at any point during the extended incident.

The Gaming Control Board cited Caesars for violating Nevada Gaming Commission Regulations 5.011(1) and (10), noting the casino "failed to immediately recognize a potential compromise to game protection and patron safety and failed to immediately take any remedial action."

The complaint seeks disciplinary action against Caesars, including potential fines of up to $100,000 per violation for first-time offenses or up to $250,000 for subsequent violations. The Gaming Commission also maintains the authority to take action against Caesars' gaming licenses.

The case highlights Nevada gaming regulators' emphasis on proper casino operations and their mandate to ensure gaming activities are conducted with appropriate standards of decorum while protecting public safety and the industry's reputation.

The Office Bar – Free Beer

The Nevada Gaming Control Board filed a complaint against Diana June Reed, owner of The Office bar in Elko, Nevada, alleging multiple violations of gaming regulations and license conditions.

The case stems from a September 2008 license condition prohibiting Larry Dale Nielsen from involvement in business operations until he received gaming commission approval. Despite this restriction, Nielsen was observed performing various unauthorized activities at the establishment.

In August 2009, gaming agents witnessed Nielsen pouring himself free draft beers, operating the cash register, handling money from patrons, and leaving contact information for staff to reach him about bar problems.

The violations continued into 2010. In May, Elko police responded to reports of an intoxicated bartender and found Nielsen drunk while serving drinks. With no other bartenders available, police ordered the bar closed. Nielsen later told the police chief he was Reed's only bartender at The Office.

The situation escalated in June when Nielsen was caught serving alcohol to an underage person during a police compliance check. He became belligerent with officers when confronted. Later the same day, another bartender, Janice Gibson, also served alcohol to an underage customer.

On June 19, after another underage serving incident, the Elko police chief ordered The Office closed. Hours later, officers found the bar still operating with Nielsen present. When police attempted to stop him, Nielsen fled into the bar and resisted arrest. Officers discovered intoxicated bartender Gibson and multiple patrons inside. Despite being warned, Reed was later observed continuing to serve drinks.

The complaint also cites Reed's failure to comply with license conditions requiring timely filing of key employee applications. An initial incomplete application was submitted late in November 2008, with missing information not received until February 2009. After the key employee left in July 2009, Reed failed to submit a new application as required within 60 days.

The Gaming Control Board seeks fines and potential action against The Office's gaming license for these violations of state gaming regulations and unsuitable business operations.

The Office Bar in Elko - Underage Service

The Nevada Gaming Control Board filed a complaint against Diana June Reed, owner of The Office bar in Elko, Nevada, citing multiple violations of gaming regulations and license conditions.

The troubles began in September 2008 when The Office received a two-year limited restricted gaming license with specific conditions. A key requirement prohibited Larry Dale Nielsen from any involvement in business operations until he received gaming commission approval. Reed agreed Nielsen would only handle maintenance tasks.

However, surveillance in August 2009 caught Nielsen engaging in prohibited activities. He was observed pouring himself free drinks, handling cash transactions, operating the register, and leaving his contact information for staff - all violations of his restricted status.

The situation escalated in May 2010 when Elko Police responded to reports of an intoxicated bartender at The Office. Officers found Nielsen drunk while serving as bartender and ordered the establishment closed. In a later conversation with the Police Chief, Nielsen claimed he was Reed's only bartender.

Further violations occurred in June 2010. Police spotted Nielsen tending a sidewalk bar owned by The Office. The same day, during two separate compliance checks, both Nielsen and another bartender, Janice Gibson, served alcohol to underage persons working with law enforcement.

The problems peaked on June 19, 2010, when The Office defied a police order to close. After multiple underage serving incidents, the Chief of Police shut down the establishment. Later night, officers found the bar still operating with patrons inside. When confronted, Nielsen fled into the bar, resisted officers, and was arrested. Gibson, heavily intoxicated, refused to leave and required police escort.

The complaint also details The Office's failure to maintain proper key employee documentation. The establishment missed deadlines for filing required applications and operated without a designated key employee for approximately two years.

The Gaming Control Board seeks monetary fines for each violation and potential action against The Office's gaming license. The case highlights the strict oversight of Nevada's gaming industry and the serious consequences of regulatory non-compliance.

Half Shell Gaming Properties - Owner Transfers

The Nevada Gaming Control Board filed a complaint against Half Shell LLC and Half Shell 2 LLC, along with several individuals, for allegedly transferring ownership interests without required regulatory approval.

According to the complaint, Trevett Jay Williams submitted ownership verification forms in August 2009 indicating significant changes in both gaming properties' ownership structure. The forms revealed Raymond Todd Stratton had transferred his entire 25% stake in both Half Shell locations to The James K. Johnson Gaming Properties Trust and/or James Charles Wayne. Additionally, Williams transferred 15% of his own 25% interest to the same entities.

The unauthorized transfers resulted in a dramatic shift in ownership percentages. The new structure showed The James K. Johnson Gaming Properties Trust holding 37.5%, Williams retaining 10%, James Charles Wayne controlling 52.5%, and Stratton's interest reduced to zero in both properties.

The Gaming Control Board sent multiple written notices to Williams and both Half Shell entities between September 2009 and January 2010, explaining the transfers required pre-approval from the Nevada Gaming Commission. Despite repeated requests, the companies and their principals failed to submit the necessary applications by March 17, 2010.

The complaint outlines two counts of violations, one for each Half Shell location, citing breaches of Nevada Revised Statute 463.5733 and Gaming Commission regulations. These regulations explicitly prohibit the sale, transfer, or disposition of any interest in gaming license holders without advance Commission approval.

The Board seeks monetary fines for each violation and potential action against the gaming licenses held by the respondents. The case underscores Nevada's strict oversight of gaming ownership changes, designed to maintain industry integrity and public trust.

Both Half Shell properties operate under restricted gaming licenses in Henderson, Nevada - one located on East Horizon Ridge Parkway and the other on South Eastern Avenue.

Brandywine Bookmaking - Race Wagers

In a complaint filed by the Nevada Gaming Control Board, Brandywine Bookmaking LLC, operating as Lucky's, was charged with accepting unauthorized race wagers at two of its satellite locations in 2009.

The violations came to light after Brandywine self-reported the incidents to the Board's Tax and License Division in October 2009. The company discovered it had accepted illegal race book wagers at its operations in Whiskey Pete's Hotel & Casino and the Pioneer Hotel and Gambling Hall.

Between August and October 2009, Brandywine's Pioneer Hotel location accepted 168 Twin Quinella race wagers totaling $2,320, with winnings of $2,240. The same location processed an additional 10 Breeders' Cup future race wagers in November 2009, amounting to $77. The company lacked proper licensing to accept race book wagers at Pioneer Hotel.

At Whiskey Pete's, where Brandywine had stopped accepting pari-mutuel wagers in late 2008, the company processed seven Breeders' Cup future race wagers in May and November 2009, totaling $180. By failing to pay required annual and quarterly fees after ceasing pari-mutuel operations, Brandywine effectively lost its license to operate a race book at this location.

The Board emphasized neither host location - Whiskey Pete's or Pioneer Hotel - bore any responsibility for the violations. This marked Brandywine's first disciplinary action from the Board.

The complaint cited violations of Nevada Revised Statute 463.160(1) and Nevada Gaming Commission Regulation 22.020(1), which require proper licensing for race book operations. The Board requested monetary fines for each violation and potential action against Brandywine's license.

State Gaming Control Board Chairman Dennis Neilander signed the complaint, seeking relief through the Nevada Gaming Commission's disciplinary process.

Gaming Commission Files Complaint Against Treasure Island Over Improper Detention

The Nevada Gaming Commission filed a complaint against Treasure Island, LLC in July 2010, following an incident where casino security improperly detained a patron and failed to follow required reporting procedures.

According to the complaint, the incident occurred on November 10, 2009, when a patron playing mini-baccarat placed a $500 wager. After the dealer dealt the cards but before they were exposed, the patron attempted to withdraw his bet and left the table with his chips.

Casino security intercepted the patron before he could exit the premises. Officers physically detained him and escorted him to a security holding room, where they informed him he would be going to jail. Security personnel searched the patron and confiscated all money and chips from his pockets. A casino shift manager removed five $100 chips from the patron's possession.

The casino subsequently released the patron and banned him from the property. However, Treasure Island failed to notify the Gaming Control Board's Enforcement Division or any law enforcement agency about the detention, which constituted a citizen's arrest under Nevada law.

The Gaming Control Board alleges these actions violated multiple state statutes and gaming regulations, including:

- NRS 171.178 regarding proper procedures for citizen's arrests
- NRS 171.1235 concerning casino detention policies
- Nevada Gaming Commission Regulation 5.055 requiring immediate notification of gaming law violations

The complaint emphasizes the casino's responsibility to maintain suitable operations protecting "public health, safety, morals, good order and general welfare" of Nevada residents. It notes licensees must comply with all state laws and regulations or face disciplinary action.

The Gaming Control Board seeks monetary fines for each violation and potential action against Treasure Island's gaming licenses. The exact penalties will be determined by the Gaming Commission within parameters defined by NRS 463.310(4).

This case highlights the strict regulatory framework governing Nevada casinos and the serious consequences for failing to follow proper security and reporting procedures, even when dealing with suspected gaming violations.

Champagnes Cafe - Unlicensed Operations

The Nevada Gaming Control Board filed a complaint against C & T, Inc., operating as Champagnes Cafe, alleging multiple violations of state gaming regulations and corporate laws.

The Las Vegas establishment, located at 3557 South Maryland Parkway, came under scrutiny after Ralph Louis Guarino failed to maintain proper licensing as the personal representative of the

Estate of Charles Guarino, which holds a 37.5% interest in the business.

According to the complaint, Guarino's temporary license to represent the estate expired on March 18, 2010, despite multiple warnings from the Gaming Control Board. Officials sent six written notifications between September 2009 and February 2010, including certified mail Guarino personally signed.

The Board's efforts to work through Guarino's attorney proved unsuccessful, with the attorney eventually withdrawing representation due to Guarino's lack of communication. While Guarino maintains his individual 37.5% licensed interest in Champagnes, his non-responsiveness makes him "unsuitable to be a gaming licensee," the complaint states.

The troubles deepened when Champagnes failed to file required annual paperwork with the Nevada Secretary of State. The company defaulted on January 1, 2009, and by January 2010, the state revoked its charter and right to conduct business. Despite this revocation, the establishment continued operating and offering gaming activities.

In a third count, regulators suggest the business might now be operating as an unlicensed partnership or sole proprietorship involving Thomas Francis Ridolfi, Ralph Louis Guarino, and the Estate of Charles Guarino.

The Gaming Control Board seeks monetary penalties and potential action against the establishment's gaming licenses. The case highlights Nevada's strict oversight of gaming operations and requirements for proper licensing and corporate compliance.

Ridolfi, who holds a 25% ownership stake, serves as president, secretary, treasurer, and director of the company. The complaint will proceed to the Nevada Gaming Commission for further action.

Wild Game NG's Siena Hotel - Bankroll

The Nevada Gaming Commission filed an 18-count complaint against Wild Game NG, LLC, operator of the Siena Hotel Spa & Casino in Reno, revealing widespread regulatory violations and financial irregularities spanning from 2007 to 2010.

The company failed to maintain minimum bankroll requirements for 33 out of 36 days between November 2009 and January 2010, and again for 39 out of 65 days from April to June 2010, according to the complaint.

The casino's troubles extended beyond bankroll issues. Wild Game NG missed multiple fee payments, including estimated gaming fees due in April, May, and June 2010. The company also failed to pay its quarterly nonrestricted operation fee and annual fees by the June 30, 2010 deadline.

Financial reporting problems plagued the operation. The casino's slot statistical analysis reports from May 2007 through September 2008 proved unreliable due to mishandling of free play non-cashable wagering credits. A failure in the IGT EZ-Pay ticketing system further compromised reporting accuracy.

The commission uncovered serious security breaches when reviewing surveillance footage from January 2010. In one instance, a lead graveyard security officer inserted a document into an empty blackjack table drop box before placement. Table game supervisors were caught using pre-signed inventory forms without proper verification.

Perhaps most concerning, the casino granted unauthorized administrative access to its systems. James Sinclair and David Graham of OnSite Consulting received privileges equal to the IT director between November 2009 and January 2010, despite not being registered with the Gaming Control Board or authorized vendors.

The complaint also cited the casino for failing to submit required audited financial statements, internal auditor reports, and other mandatory documentation. These violations expose Wild Game NG to potential fines and disciplinary action against its gaming license.

Barney Ng, the sole member of Siena, hired OnSite Consulting in November 2009 and granted them complete management control, but none of the consulting firm's personnel were properly registered with gaming authorities.

The Gaming Control Board is seeking monetary penalties for each violation and possible action against Wild Game NG's gaming license. The case highlights the strict regulatory environment surrounding Nevada's gaming industry and the serious consequences of non-compliance.

Dakota Convenience - Selling Drugs

The Nevada Gaming Control Board filed a complaint against Worku Y. Berhanu, owner of Dakota Convenience Store in Las Vegas, for selling and possessing a controlled substance at his restricted gaming establishment.

Las Vegas Metropolitan Police conducted surveillance of Dakota Convenience Store on Sierra Vista Drive in May 2008 after receiving tips about the sale of Khat, a controlled substance, from the premises. Officers observed multiple customers leaving the store with black plastic bags containing Khat on May 1 and May 13.

During a search warrant execution on May 15, 2008, police discovered several bags of Khat, a green leafy substance, hidden in the store's beer cooler. Berhanu admitted the Khat belonged to him, claiming it was for personal use.

Police arrested Berhanu and charged him with felony possession of a controlled substance. He later pleaded guilty to a reduced misdemeanor charge of Possession of Dangerous Drugs not to be Introduced into Interstate Commerce in May 2009.

The Gaming Control Board's complaint alleges two counts of violations. Count One charges Berhanu with failing to meet gaming license standards by selling and distributing Khat from his gaming establishment. Count Two focuses on his possession of the controlled substance on the premises.

Both counts cite violations of Nevada gaming regulations requiring licensees to maintain proper standards and avoid actions bringing discredit to the state's gaming industry. The Board seeks monetary fines and potential action against Berhanu's gaming license.

The case highlights Nevada's strict oversight of gaming establishments and requirements for licensees to operate in accordance with state laws and regulations. The Gaming Commission will determine appropriate penalties based on the Board's complaint.

Grand Slam Market - Agreement

The Nevada Gaming Control Board filed a complaint against Paul J. Nemeth, operator of the Grand Slam Market in Fallon, Nevada, alleging multiple regulatory violations spanning over a decade of operations.

The complaint outlines how Nemeth, licensed since August 1996 as the sole proprietor of Grand Slam Market, entered into an undisclosed "participation agreement" with Stillwater Gaming, LLC in March 1998. This agreement allowed Stillwater Gaming to operate slot machines and receive a percentage of net wins from the gaming devices.

In March 1999, Nemeth transferred ownership of the Grand Slam Market property to the Nemeth Family Trust without notifying gaming authorities. The complaint notes Nemeth continued representing himself as the 100% owner of the market as recently as August 2009.

The Board's investigation revealed the market's actual operations differed significantly from licensing records. Prior to March 2007, Stillwater Convenience Stores Inc., with Nemeth as sole officer and shareholder, operated the business. After March 2007, C & D Interests Inc., owned by Cheryl and Dennis McCormick, took over operations through a lease agreement with Nemeth.

The complaint lists four distinct violations:

Count One accuses Nemeth of failing to report Stillwater Gaming's profit-sharing arrangement to the Board quarterly, violating Gaming Commission regulations.

Count Two cites Nemeth's failure to notify the Board about transferring property ownership to his family trust.

Count Three alleges Nemeth made untrue statements in his license application by claiming sole proprietorship when Stillwater Convenience Stores Inc. actually operated the business.

Count Four charges Nemeth with illegally operating slot machines without being a licensed slot route operator, as he placed gaming devices at Grand Slam Market while others ran the business.

The Gaming Control Board seeks monetary fines for each violation and potential action against Nemeth's gaming licenses. The case highlights the Commission's strict oversight of gaming operations and ownership structures in Nevada.

The matter awaits a hearing before the Nevada Gaming Commission, where Nemeth will have an opportunity to respond to these allegations of regulatory non-compliance spanning from 1996 to 2010.

Fred's Tavern 2 - Unpaid $300 Patron Dispute

The Nevada Gaming Control Board filed a complaint against KRS Enterprises, Inc., operating as Fred's Tavern 2, and Kurt L. Schoen for failing to pay a patron dispute in a timely manner, despite multiple orders to do so.

The case stems from a March 5, 2009 Board hearing involving a promotional dispute between Fred's Tavern 2 and patron Michael Pascarella. The Board ordered Fred's to pay Pascarella $300 within 20 days.

Three months later, in June 2009, the Board's hearing examiner discovered Pascarella had not received his payment. When contacted, Fred's Operations Manager claimed a check had been sent to the patron.

The situation escalated in July when the hearing examiner, learning the payment remained outstanding, instructed Fred's to stop payment on the alleged check and issue a new one directly to the examiner. By August 13, neither Pascarella nor the hearing examiner had received any payment.

A Board Enforcement Division agent investigated the matter on August 14, 2009. The Operations Manager again insisted Mr. Schoen had issued and mailed a check. Later the same day, the Operations Manager delivered a $300 check to the Board.

The investigation revealed Fred's never issued or mailed the initial check, contrary to the Operations Manager's statements in June and August 2009.

The Gaming Control Board's complaint cites violations of Nevada law requiring licensees to pay patron claims within 20 days of a Board decision. The complaint also alleges Fred's failed to exercise sound judgment and maintain suitable operations methods, potentially damaging Nevada's gaming industry reputation.

The Board seeks monetary penalties and possible action against Fred's gaming license. Under Nevada law, fines can reach $100,000 for initial violations and up to $250,000 for subsequent infractions.

Justin Moscove - Violent Assault

The Nevada Gaming Commission filed a complaint against Justin Moscove, a licensed member of FT Pub II, LLC, following a violent incident at Archie's Giant Hamburgers in Reno.

According to the complaint, on November 15, 2008, around 7:00 PM, Moscove approached Jens Morrison and struck him in the head with a closed fist. Morrison fell, hitting his head on a car's rim before landing on the ground, sustaining substantial injuries. Moscove left the scene without rendering aid and went to the Patio Bar in Reno.

Morrison required immediate medical attention and was rushed by ambulance to Renown Medical Center, where he reportedly stopped breathing, needed resuscitation, and was placed on a ventilator.

When Reno Police Officers located Moscove at the Patio Bar and questioned him about the battery, he denied any involvement and claimed he hadn't been at Archie's Giant Hamburgers. Police arrested him on November 16, 2008.

The criminal case concluded with Moscove entering a Nolo Contendere Plea to felony Battery Causing Substantial Bodily Harm and gross misdemeanor Conspiracy to Commit Battery Causing Substantial Bodily Harm. On October 2, 2009, he was found guilty of the conspiracy charge and sentenced to 12 months imprisonment with a restitution order of $276,106.25. The sentence was suspended with 36 months probation.

The Gaming Commission's complaint alleges Moscove's actions demonstrate a lack of character, honesty, and integrity required for gaming licensure. The Commission cites three specific failures: the violent assault itself, abandoning an injured person, and lying to police officers.

The complaint seeks monetary fines and potential action against Moscove's gaming license, arguing his behavior violated Nevada gaming regulations and reflected poorly on the state's gaming industry.

Morrison filed a separate civil complaint against Moscove and others on December 23, 2009, related to the incident.

Pocket Change no License

The Nevada Gaming Control Board filed a complaint against M & M Pocket Change Inc. and its president Salam Matti Razuki for failing to comply with licensing conditions at their Las Vegas establishment.

According to documents filed with the Nevada Gaming Commission on March 2, 2010, Pocket Change, located at 5020 East Tropicana Avenue, received a restricted gaming license on December 18, 2008. The Commission placed a key condition on the license: the business needed to file a key employee application within 60 days of license issuance and after any subsequent personnel changes.

The gaming license was issued on June 1, 2009. Despite this requirement, Pocket Change failed to submit the mandatory key employee application during the specified timeframe. The Board made multiple attempts to obtain compliance, sending letters to Razuki on August 3, September 2, and October 2, 2009 - with the final notice delivered by certified mail.

As of the complaint filing date, Pocket Change still had not submitted the required application. The Board cited this failure as a violation of Nevada Gaming Commission Regulation 5.011, declaring it an unsuitable method of operation.

The Gaming Control Board seeks monetary penalties under NRS 463.310(4) for each separate violation and potential additional action against Pocket Change's gaming license. The case highlights Nevada's strict regulatory framework for gaming establishments and the state's commitment to maintaining compliance with licensing conditions.

The complaint was submitted by Attorney General Catherine Cortez Masto and Senior Deputy Attorney General Michael P. Somps on behalf of the State Gaming Control Board.

Thomas P. Berry - Disclosure Failure

The Nevada Gaming Commission filed a complaint against The Thomas P. Berry Special Trust and Thomas Patrick Berry for failing to notify regulators about a property ownership change related to their gaming operations.

According to the complaint filed in February 2010, the Commission discovered during an investigation the real property housing Ballpark Market, LLC had been sold to Day Investments, LLC on January 30, 2009. Thomas Berry knew about the sale but failed to inform the Gaming Control Board as required by regulations.

The discovery came after Berry filed applications in June 2009 to transfer 100% ownership interest in Ballpark Market to James Earl Day and Elizabeth Rose Day. During the Board's review of these applications, investigators uncovered the earlier undisclosed property sale.

The complaint notes Berry had received a previous violation letter in October 2008 for a similar failure - not notifying the Board when the same property was sold to Moana M & V, LLC.

Nevada gaming regulations require licensees to immediately notify the Board upon learning about any change or contemplated change in ownership of premises where licensed gaming occurs. The

Commission considers such disclosure failures "unsuitable methods of operation" and grounds for disciplinary action.

The Gaming Control Board seeks monetary fines and potential action against Berry's gaming licenses. Berry holds multiple gaming interests through his trust, including shares in Berry Properties Inc., Winner's Gaming Inc., Berry's Casino Inc., Carson Plains Casino LLC, and Silver Strike Casino LLC.

The case highlights Nevada's strict oversight of gaming property transactions, aimed at maintaining "public confidence and trust" through rigorous regulation of all aspects of licensed gaming operations.

Harrah's Las Vegas - Sports Bet Cancellations

A complaint filed by the Nevada Gaming Control Board alleges Harrah's Las Vegas Casino Hotel improperly voided three sports wagers and discriminated against a patron based on player rating levels.

The incident occurred on April 12, 2008, when a patron placed three $550 wagers at the Harrah's sports book. The patron used lines from an "Overnight Lines Pro Basketball" wagering sheet distributed by a Harrah's affiliate. Though the lines weren't displayed on the sports book boards, they remained accessible in the computer system.

A sports book supervisor approved all three wagers after the system flagged them for review. The patron funded the $1,650 total using a $1,050 winning ticket and $600 cash. However, after checking the patron's player rating history, the supervisor abruptly retrieved the tickets, voided the bets, and returned the money - all without the patron's consent.

When the patron objected, the supervisor suggested returning in the morning or placing the wagers at Caesars Palace instead.

The Gaming Control Board cited two major violations in its complaint. First, Harrah's breached Nevada Gaming Commission Regulation 22.115 by unilaterally rescinding wagers without prior written approval from the Board's Chairman.

The second violation centered on unlawful discrimination. During interviews, Board agents discovered the supervisor voided the bets because the patron's player rating level wasn't deemed high enough for overnight lines - a practice prohibited by Nevada law. Under NRS 463.0129(e), public access to gaming activities cannot be restricted except as specifically allowed by the Legislature.

The Board seeks monetary fines for each violation and potential action against Harrah's gaming license. The complaint represents another example of Nevada regulators' commitment to ensuring fair and open access to gaming, regardless of a patron's player rating or status.

Mini Mart Owner - Not the Real Owner

The Nevada Gaming Commission filed a complaint against Sam Elias Hamika, a sole proprietorship owner operating two Kwiky Mini Mart locations in Las Vegas, for multiple gaming license violations. The complaint, filed in December 2009, centers on unauthorized business transfers and failure to report property ownership changes.

According to the complaint, Hamika transferred all rights and interests in his gaming operations at both mini mart locations - one on North Eastern Avenue and another on East Tropicana Avenue -

to the Hamika Family Trust before May 2009. The trust, managed by Hamika and his wife Soondis as trustees and beneficiaries, began operating gaming activities without obtaining proper licensing.

The Commission alleges Hamika never notified the Gaming Control Board about no longer being the operator of the businesses. By allowing the trust to run gaming operations without a license, Hamika violated Nevada state law NRS 463.160. The complaint notes he also breached NRS 463.161 by continuing to hold a restricted gaming license while not operating the primary businesses.

In a second count, regulators uncovered a series of unreported property transfers dating back to 1995. When first approved for gaming operations at the North Eastern location, the property belonged to Burgundy Company. The land transferred to Hamika and his wife as joint tenants in 1997, and later to the family trust in 2006. Hamika failed to notify the Gaming Control Board about any of these property ownership changes, violating Nevada Gaming Commission Regulation 3.020(4).

The Gaming Control Board seeks monetary fines for each violation and potential action against Hamika's gaming licenses. The complaint emphasizes license holders must maintain compliance with all regulations and cannot claim ignorance as an excuse for violations.

The case highlights Nevada's strict oversight of gaming operations, where licenses are considered revocable privileges requiring continuous compliance with state regulations to protect public interests and maintain industry integrity.

Palms Casino Resort and Tournament Operations

The Nevada Gaming Control Board filed a complaint against Fiesta Palms, LLC, operating as Palms Casino Resort, for multiple violations related to poker tournaments held at the Las Vegas property in 2007.

In August 2007, the Palms hosted a poker tournament organized by Michael Eakman & Associates (MEA) to benefit the Jewish Community Center of Southern Nevada. MEA received 75% of the tournament profits while failing to register with the Gaming Control Board as required by state law. The casino failed to verify MEA's registration status before allowing the event to proceed.

The situation worsened when MEA delayed remitting the donation to the Jewish Community Center for over four months after the tournament concluded.

A second incident occurred in October 2007 when the Palms hosted a poker tournament organized by the United States Poker League (USPL). The USPL, also unregistered with the Gaming Board, collected entry fees and was responsible for prize payouts. At the tournament's conclusion, the USPL lacked sufficient funds to cover all prizes.

Twenty-seven winners received half their prizes in cash and half in post-dated checks for November 1, 2007. When participants attempted to cash these checks, 22 were returned for insufficient funds, totaling $450,416 in unpaid prizes. The Palms ultimately paid all outstanding prizes from its own funds.

The Gaming Control Board cited five counts against the Palms:
- Allowing an unregistered company (MEA) to conduct a tournament
- Failing to exercise proper discretion and judgment regarding the MEA tournament

- Allowing an unregistered company (USPL) to conduct a tournament
- Failing to ensure immediate prize payment as required by gaming regulations
- Failing to exercise proper discretion and judgment regarding the USPL tournament

The Board seeks monetary fines and potential action against the Palms' gaming license. The complaint emphasizes the casino's responsibility to maintain suitable operations and protect public confidence in Nevada's gaming industry.

The case highlights the critical importance of proper tournament oversight and regulatory compliance in Nevada's gaming operations. The Board's complaint underscores how operational failures can potentially damage the state's gaming reputation and industry stability.

Comstock Games, Inc. Slot Machine Violations

The Nevada State Gaming Control Board launched an investigation into Comstock Games, Inc. after receiving reports of persistently malfunctioning slot machines at multiple Reno-area locations.

The investigation, initiated in May 2008, revealed a pattern of neglect at Spirit Gas and Grocery in Reno, where agents found four out of five slot machines out of order. Over the next week, inspectors documented machines cycling between complete failure and functionality, with all five machines breaking down on May 18.

Spirit's owner reported Comstock Games failed to maintain adequate coin levels for sustained play. Dan Meyer, the company's majority shareholder and president, allegedly ignored multiple phone messages requesting service.

The problems extended beyond Spirit. At Coney Island Bar in Sparks, agents discovered all five slot machines powered down in October 2008, with three marked as malfunctioning. The bar's owner had unsuccessfully attempted to contact Meyer for repairs since October 3.

The situation deteriorated further at Big Horn Bar and Grill in Reno, where inspectors found all six machines non-operational in October 2008. One machine had remained broken for approximately a month, despite a Technology Division directive to fix a screen adjustment issue.

Board agents documented additional violations at Shamrock Grocery and Deli and the General Store, including missing operator identification labels and non-working telephone numbers on service tags.

The Gaming Control Board filed two counts against Comstock Games. The first count cites violations of multiple gaming regulations, including failure to maintain suitable conditions and conduct proper gaming operations. The second count addresses the company's failure to properly label machines with valid contact information.

The complaint seeks monetary fines for each violation and potential action against Comstock's gaming licenses. The case highlights the Gaming Commission's mandate to maintain public confidence in Nevada's gaming industry through strict regulation of operators and equipment.

Meyer's repeated failure to respond to service calls and maintain proper machine operations across multiple venues demonstrates a pattern of negligence spanning several months in 2008 and early 2009, according to the complaint.

The case now moves to the Nevada Gaming Commission for further action.

Searchlight Casino – Records

The Nevada Gaming Commission filed a comprehensive complaint against the Searchlight Nugget Casino, highlighting years of operational deficiencies and regulatory violations.

The Board's investigation revealed persistent issues despite previous violation letters sent in February 2007 and October 2005. The latest examination, conducted in May and June 2007, uncovered widespread problems with record-keeping, security procedures, and financial controls.

Among the most serious violations, investigators found unauthorized access to sensitive gaming keys, improper handling of currency drops, and failure to maintain accurate slot machine statistics. In one instance, the casino allowed a single person to count vault contents, violating the requirement for dual verification.

The complaint details troubling financial discrepancies, including unexplained withdrawals of $5,852 and $2,000 in 2005 and 2006 respectively. Investigators also discovered significant adjustments to slot machine revenue reports, with increases of $34,031 in April 2005 and $3,200 in September 2005, made without supporting documentation.

Security protocols showed alarming gaps. Full coin drop buckets were left unsecured outside the count room, and duplicate keys were stored improperly, allowing unauthorized access. The casino failed to perform required quarterly tests of currency counters and weight scales.

Financial reporting irregularities continued throughout the investigation period. The casino neglected to report a $77,094 capital contribution and a $43,817 loan for insurance premiums to the Gaming Board. It also failed to maintain minimum bankroll calculations since May 2006.

Record-keeping deficiencies extended to the casino's live entertainment revenue, which was improperly combined with non-entertainment income, making it impossible to distinguish between the two revenue streams.

The Gaming Commission seeks monetary penalties for each violation and possible action against the casino's gaming licenses. The case underscores the Commission's commitment to maintaining strict oversight of Nevada's gaming operations and ensuring compliance with regulatory standards.

The complaint serves as a reminder to all gaming establishments of the importance of maintaining proper controls and following regulatory requirements. The Commission will determine appropriate penalties based on the severity and number of violations.

Planet Hollywood - Nightclub Operations

The Nevada State Gaming Control Board has filed a comprehensive complaint against Planet Hollywood Resort & Casino, citing multiple violations related to its nightclub Prive. The complaint stems from a 2007 agreement between the casino and The Opium Group to operate a nightclub on the premises.

Prior to the agreement, in February 2006, the Gaming Board had warned all nonrestricted gaming licensees about nightclub-related incidents. The warning specifically addressed concerns about excessive intoxication, drug distribution, violence, involvement of minors, and handling of incapacitated individuals.

According to the complaint, Planet Hollywood management knew of numerous concerning incidents but failed to take appropriate action. The casino's responsibilities extended to all activities on its premises, including those at Prive.

The complaint outlines a pattern of troubling behavior. Prive staff regularly removed over-intoxicated patrons, leaving them unattended in the casino. Multiple guests required hospitalization for alcohol overconsumption, while others were found using controlled substances within the venue.

Several patrons alleged both physical and sexual assault by Prive employees. The nightclub also faced citations from Clark County Department of Business License for allowing topless and lewd activity, plus failing to cooperate with county agents.

The situation worsened after Prive's opening. Emergency medical service calls at Planet Hollywood jumped significantly - from 61 calls in the year before Prive opened to 106 calls in the following eight months. Police responses also increased dramatically, with notable spikes in assault, fighting, and narcotics-related incidents.

Law enforcement reported significant prostitution activity around Prive, which Planet Hollywood allegedly failed to address. The casino also neglected to screen Prive employees' criminal records or exercise proper oversight of staff.

The Gaming Board's complaint emphasizes Planet Hollywood's lack of control over its leased premises. The agreement with Prive provided insufficient oversight, essentially shifting responsibility to gaming regulators. Even Planet Hollywood's security officers needed Prive employee escorts to enter the nightclub during business hours.

Despite having authority to terminate the agreement if Prive jeopardized Planet Hollywood's licenses or business, casino management never exercised this option - even though security reports documented most incidents.

The Gaming Commission will now determine potential penalties, which could include fines and action against Planet Hollywood's gaming licenses. The case underscores the gaming industry's strict regulatory environment and licensees' responsibility to maintain suitable operations throughout their properties.

Poker Palace Betting Scheme

In a sweeping investigation conducted jointly with U.S. Immigration and Customs Enforcement, the Nevada Gaming Board uncovered extensive violations at Poker Palace's race book operation during 2006. The investigation revealed a sophisticated scheme involving unlicensed bookmakers who were laying off wagers through the establishment's race book.

According to the complaint, Poker Palace actively courted the illegal bookmaking group's business through an elaborate contest scheme designed to circumvent state gaming laws. The establishment offered an off-track pari-mutuel contest with a steep $2,500 entry fee—far above their typical customer's $2-$5 average bet per race.

The investigation exposed five major violations. First, Poker Palace provided unlawful rebates on pari-mutuel wagers through a contest serving as a front for the rebate scheme. The contest required minimum weekly wagers of $200,000 from the group—double the casino's typical monthly handle of $100,000.

Second, the establishment illegally shared pari-mutuel revenue without Nevada Gaming Commission approval. The contest guaranteed the bookmaking group a percentage of gaming revenue through prize pools tied to betting volume.

In the third violation, Poker Palace knowingly accepted wagers from messenger bettors working for the unlicensed bookmakers. The fourth count cited the establishment for paying winning tickets to individuals who hadn't placed the original bets.

The final violation targeted Marvin E. Coleman, the sole trustee-beneficiary of the trust owning Poker Palace. The Board determined Coleman failed to adequately monitor race book operations during the period when illegal bookmakers operated freely in his establishment.

The investigation revealed few legitimate participants entered these contests beyond the illegal bookmaking group. With four prizes available and typically only four contestants, nearly every participant walked away with winnings—effectively guaranteeing returns on their wagering activity.

These violations constituted unsuitable operation methods under Nevada gaming regulations, leading to disciplinary action against both the establishment and its ownership. The case highlighted significant failures in regulatory compliance and oversight at one of Nevada's licensed gaming establishments.

St. Tropez Operations - Delegation of Power

In a complex case spanning nearly two decades, the Nevada Gaming Control Board filed multiple counts of violations against St. Tropez Convenience Mart and St. Tropez Liquor Store operations and its stakeholders.

The story begins in 1990 when the Nevada Gaming Commission approved Tropez to operate as St. Tropez Convenience Mart, with Richard Carl Ritzo, Kimberly Ann Antonacci, and Anthony Joseph Antonacci, Sr. as equal shareholders. Two years later, the commission approved their liquor store operation under similar ownership structure.

A series of significant ownership changes occurred following Anthony Joseph Antonacci's death in 2001. His widow, Bernice Elizabeth Antonacci, inherited his share through probate, but failed to file an executrix application within the required 30-day period. The commission eventually approved her role in 2002.

The Board outlined four major counts of violations:

Count One focuses on leadership transitions. Bernice Elizabeth Antonacci became president in June 2007 but filed her licensing application 106 days late. The Board cited this as an unsuitable method of operation.

Count Two details improper officer appointments from a February 2008 stockholders' meeting. The company elected Richard Carl Ritzo as President/Director, Joellen Darling Ritzo as Treasurer/Director, and Edward Antonacci as Secretary/Director - none properly licensed for these positions.

Count Three addresses unauthorized delegation of power. In February 2008, Bernice Elizabeth Antonacci appointed her son, Edward Antonacci, to exercise all her powers without proper gaming board approval.

Count Four concerns unauthorized trust formation and ownership transfer. Following Richard and Joellen Darling Ritzo's 2002 divorce, their joint one-third interest split into individual one-sixth shares. Joellen later formed an unlicensed family trust to hold her interest.

The Gaming Control Board seeks monetary fines for each violation and potential action against existing licenses through the Nevada Gaming Commission.

Las Vegas Gaming Inc. - Required Reserves

Las Vegas Gaming Inc. (LVGI) faced disciplinary action after failing to maintain required financial reserves and violating multiple Nevada Gaming Commission regulations during the spring of 2008.

The violations stem from a 2006 agreement when LVGI received permission to use a periodic payment plan for its Nevada Numbers jackpot payouts. Under this arrangement, LVGI partnered with another Nevada gaming licensee to bankroll $2.9 million of its jackpot obligations, while LVGI maintained the remaining required reserves.

Financial troubles emerged on March 31, 2008, when investigators discovered LVGI's restricted account fell below mandatory levels. The situation worsened as the company's bankroll dropped below minimum requirements on both April 23 and June 2, 2008.

Adding to the company's regulatory woes, LVGI failed to notify the Gaming Control Board about these bankroll deficiencies - a clear violation of state gaming regulations requiring immediate disclosure of such shortfalls.

The Gaming Control Board filed three separate counts against LVGI. The first addresses the March restricted account deficiency, while the second and third counts focus on the April and June bankroll violations and subsequent failure to report these issues to regulators.

The filing marks a significant challenge for LVGI, coming less than two years after the Nevada Gaming Commission revised its bankroll formula in February 2006. The company had received special permission to operate under a modified payment plan in June of the same year.

According to regulatory documents, LVGI's troubles constitute an "unsuitable method of operation" - a serious designation in Nevada's gaming industry. These violations place the company's gaming licenses at risk and expose it to substantial financial penalties under NRS 463.310(4).

Carson City Laundromat - No Employee Supervision

In a case highlighting Nevada's strict gaming oversight, a Carson City laundromat faced multiple violations for improper operation of its restricted gaming license and unauthorized alcohol sales to minors. The Laundry Lounge, initially licensed in December 1996 to Dung So Truong and Ly Siek Truong as joint owners, received approval to operate six gaming devices with the explicit condition requiring a full-time attendant on duty whenever machines were available for play.

The business began accumulating violations in 2003 when the owners formed the Laundry Lounge Corporation without obtaining proper gaming licenses. Despite the corporate restructuring, neither the corporation nor its officers secured the necessary approvals from the Nevada Gaming Commission to continue operating gaming devices.

The situation escalated on May 15, 2008, when a non-employee, Nelson Alberto-Lemus, was left in charge of the establishment. During his unauthorized supervision, Alberto-Lemus sold alcohol to an underage decoy during a compliance check by the Carson City

Sheriff's Office. The gaming devices remained available for play during this period, violating multiple regulations.

The consequences were swift. By June 19, 2008, the Carson City Board of Supervisors revoked the establishment's packaged beer and wine license. The Nevada Gaming Control Board filed a complaint citing three major violations:

1. Operating without proper corporate gaming licenses since 2003
2. Allowing alcohol sales to minors
3. Failing to maintain required employee supervision of gaming operations

The Gaming Control Board recommended monetary penalties for each violation and potential action against the establishment's gaming licenses. The case underscores Nevada's commitment to maintaining strict oversight of gaming operations, even in establishments with restricted licenses.

The Board emphasized the Truongs' "unsuitable method of operation" in their complaint, pointing to multiple regulatory breaches spanning several years. This case serves as a reminder of Nevada's rigorous gaming industry standards, where even small operations must maintain strict compliance with state regulations.

The Black Book

Today's Black Book includes individuals from various backgrounds, from professional card counters to tech-savvy advantage players. The criteria for inclusion remains strict - candidates must meet at least one of four specific conditions: conviction of gaming-related crimes, violation of gaming laws, possession of a notorious reputation, or violation of casino exclusion orders.

The Gray List serves as a preliminary step, allowing casinos to monitor suspicious individuals before considering permanent exclusion. This temporary status provides both casinos and patrons an opportunity to address concerns before escalation to permanent ban status. Several current Gray List members remain under observation for suspected advantage play techniques and coordinated team efforts to beat casino games.

Recently this notorious "Black Book" of banned casino patrons expanded to 36 members with the addition of Shaun Joseph Benward, a self-proclaimed magician and illusionist from Mississippi. The Commission's unanimous vote highlighted their commitment to maintaining casino integrity and protecting gaming establishments from sophisticated cheating schemes.

The Black Book, officially known as Nevada's List of Excluded Persons, serves as the gaming industry's ultimate deterrent against casino cheats and undesirable individuals. Created in the 1960s, this list emerged during a period when organized crime posed a serious threat to Nevada's gaming industry. The list includes two categories: the Black List for permanent bans and the Gray List for temporary exclusions.

Benward's inclusion followed a pattern of deceptive behavior across multiple gaming establishments. His modus operandi involved a calculated approach to roulette tables, where he would strategically position himself away from the wheel. Through carefully crafted conversations, he would build rapport with dealers before executing his scheme. His technique involved disputed late bets and manipulated confusion about chip placement, often supported by accomplices who corroborated his false claims.

The scope of Benward's activities proved extensive. In 2020 alone, nine Las Vegas casinos expelled him during July and August. His career total of 17 Nevada casino ejections, combined with convictions for roulette cheating across multiple states, made him an prime candidate for the Black Book. Gaming establishments reported substantial financial losses due to his activities.

Historical context adds perspective to this latest addition. The Black Book's most famous entry remains Frank "Lefty" Rosenthal, whose life inspired the film "Casino." Rosenthal, despite his controversial status, managed several Las Vegas casinos during the 1970s before his listing. Modern surveillance technology has made the detection of cheating more sophisticated, but determined individuals still attempt to beat the system.

Another notable figure, Richard Marcus, earned his place through elaborate cheating schemes in the 1990s. Marcus later wrote books about his methods, inadvertently helping casinos improve their security measures. Technology professional John Kane found himself Gray Listed after discovering and exploiting a software glitch in video poker machines, leading to significant casino losses before his detection.

Casino security experts emphasize the evolution of cheating methods. While traditional schemes like marked cards or loaded dice have become less common, sophisticated technology and social engineering tactics present new challenges. The Gaming Commission's vigilance through these lists helps maintain Nevada's reputation as a leader in gaming integrity.

Exclusion from Nevada casinos carries serious consequences. Banned individuals face criminal charges if found on casino property, with penalties including substantial fines and potential imprisonment. The ban extends beyond gaming areas to all casino-related venues, including restaurants, shops, and entertainment facilities within these establishments.

The Gaming Commission's recent action against Benward demonstrates their ongoing commitment to protecting Nevada's gaming industry. As surveillance technology advances and cheating methods evolve, the Black Book continues its role as a crucial tool in maintaining casino integrity. For aspiring cheats and advantaged players, the message remains clear: Nevada's gaming authorities maintain zero tolerance for those who threaten the fairness of casino operations.

These 100+ cases prove that the work of the commission is valuable, Over 1.6 billion worldwide participate in gambling activities and 80% of those in the US are estimated to gamble

The inner workings of the Nevada Gaming Commission remain a mystery—despite 81% of Nevada's revenue coming from the casinos. Their main focus might be to minimize untaxed gaming activity, but every complaint requires some investigation. Hopefully this book will be starting point for your own investigations!

Acknowledgements

Thank you to my editors at SmilingEagle Press, Cathy Phillips and Doogie Souz, for helping get this book completed with incentive and guidance.

A big thank you to Chandra who taught me how to write my first novel from one of my screenplays. Many thanks to my husband Keith who has given me love, encouragement, and constructive criticism for over fifty years.

A special thanks to my family and friends who critique my books and make comments; Laura Ailes, Gayle Higby, Amy Delk, Jennifer Ellis, Andrea Navarrette, Camille DeMoss, Jack Ross, Mark Saunders, JJ Waya, and Miss Michael.

About the Author

Sandi Jerome is a writer and graduate of UCLA's Advanced Screenwriting program. Her screenplay, ***Runaway Cricket***, is being produced as an animated musical by BlackOrb.com.

Sandi is an enrolled and blood member of the Cherokee Nation and a 2023 Native American Media Alliance fellow - twice. She hopes to get the word out about the history of her people - but in a fun and smart way. Sandi likes to create Native American characters that are memorable, engaging, and non-stereotypical. Most of her scripts have a Native American part - for many, the lead is a female, Indigenous person.

In her first NAMA TV writing fellowship, she wrote ***Technically Soccer***, a half-hour comedy about a Women's Professional Soccer team getting an AI-Robot coach. It is being developed into a TV series by Little Studio Films. Sandi is an avid women's soccer fan; she has coached, played, and refereed soccer for over twenty years.

Her middle-grade book, ***Sleep Warrior,*** about her Cherokee ancestor, is on Coverfly's Red List as the #3 Animated Manuscripts. Sandi's family is part of the Wolf Clan of the Cherokee tribe and she has written two screenplays with wolves. NOT werewolves - these wolves are real. ***Blood Moon Wolf*** (TV Pilot and Feature) was completed as part of her 2nd Native American fellowship about a wolf turning into the girl to be a spirit guide.

She grew up on an avocado farm in Escondido and was the "go to" kid to climb up high and pick the top fruit. She would then jump down into the thick pile of leaves and thought she could fly! She created young adult fantasy book, ***Kira and Henry*** - where the teen princess has to hide the secret that she can fly or be banished from the kingdom. It was a 2nd Rounder in 2023 Austin Film Festival and a 2024 Kindle Book Review finalist.

Sandi is a scientist and loves designing edible gardens and doing botany experiments. Her early fascination with science and the nearby San Onofre Nuclear Generating station inspired her to write an action script, ***Use of Deadly Force***. Her husband was a technical writer in the nuclear industry and ensured its authenticity. Sandi aims to help emerging producers and directors get their projects to the screen.

She is a native Californian, born in Santa Ana. She belonged to a Science and Technology group and helped develop a volunteer Web on Wheels program that brought email to residents of assisted living centers. This inspired her body-switching comedy, ***Time for Lily***, which was a First-Round Finalist in Script Magazine Open Door Contest.

As a former computer programmer, she has been granted two patents for software design and recently sold her software company. She wrote a Sci-Fi, thriller script, ***Last Woman***, which involves the multi-universe and technology gone awry. It was a semifinalist in Final Draft's Big Break contest in 2023.

Sandi was the first editor of Digital Dealer and wrote computer software reviews for major publications and numerous published computer guides.

As a long-time Disney fan, annual passholder and certified Disney expert. She wrote ***Pixie Dust Death*** as a young adult novel set at the Magic Kingdom and Grand Floridian. Pixie Dust Death is part of Sandi's ***Wilma Wallaby Genius Girl Detective Series*** and has 5-Star reviews and good rankings on Amazon. It is being developed into a kid's series by a UK Production company.

Sandi wrote ***Hijacked*** for producer Melissa Shevela of Helicopter Productions which is being shopped by fellow producer Autumn Bailey of AB Entertainment (*On a Wing and a Prayer* with Dennis Quaid.) Autumn is shopping two of Sandi's Hallmark-like Christmas scripts along with a faith-based RomCom. Melissa has optioned this case-file book and they are developing a procedural TV series, ***Last Hand***.

She is the author of the ***Amazing Animals of Disney's Animal Kingdom***. Trained as a feature screenwriter, Sandi has been concentrating on developing her TV projects and now has five pilots ready with 8-10 future episodes each outlined and 3 seasons planned, along with many more young adult novels. For Sandi, "***Writing is life***!"

Learn more at www.sandrajerome.com or leave comments at her publisher's Contact page, www.smilingeagle.com.

www.ingramcontent.com/pod-product-compliance
Lightning Source LLC
Chambersburg PA
CBHW072250270326
41930CB00010B/2330

* 9 7 8 1 7 3 6 0 3 4 8 7 3 *